ENJOY

They Call Me Sir

Sylvia H. Eckhardt

A STORY UNTOLD NEVER HELPS ANYONE.

(Unknown)

Dedication

To Dr. Suresh for his tireless work with this tribe.
To Vasentha for letting me write his story.
And to my husband, Loren, who gave endless
encouragement.

Acknowledgements

No book is ever the product of just one person. I am extremely grateful for the prodding of Dawn Hurley as she constantly encouraged me to write this book. Dawn's second contribution to this book was her hours of meticulous editing. Without her urging there would be only sketches and few words. Thank you, Dawn.

Without the sweet humble spirit of Dr. Suresh there would be no book. He translated many of the events that happened with Vasentha. He reached out to a group of people so shunned it was thought unimaginable by the general Indian population for him to pursue a relationship with this *Paradhi* tribe. Thank you, Suresh for listening to the still small voice of *Yeshu.*

Jim Erikson was of tremendous help in the pursuit of getting Starting Point translated into *Marathi*. He provided the resources of North Point Ministries and Global X to this project. Thank you, Jim.

Another person who was instrumental in getting this venture finished is Becky Golab, who read and reread the manuscript with advice and attention to details. Her enthusiasm kept me going. A big thank-you, Becky.

Without the permission of Vasentha, this project would never have been a reality. I'm not sure he knew what he was agreeing to, but I thank you, Vasentha, for allowing me to give your miraculous and unimaginable story to the world.

Last but not least is my husband, Loren, my forever love, who stands by me in all my unthinkable quests and says, "You can do it, honey."

Preface

Not unlike the gulf between the Samaritans and the Jews of biblical times, the Indian population and the *Paradhis* have complete and utter distain for each other. The caste system in India means that *Paradhi*, who are not really even of part of this system, are not allowed to **attend school or own land, and if they are dying, you can't call an ambulance. If they are dead, no one will touch their body.** With no running water or toilet facilities for them, it's not surprising that most *Paradhis* suffer from extremely poor health. If they live in the cities they give birth on polluted pavement and, after a lifetime of begging and struggling, most of them die on the streets.

It would be unimaginable for any Indian in the caste system to help a *Paradhi* in any way.

What is the most unthinkable thing to you? Drinking from a sewer? Becoming president? Going to the moon? This is a story of the unimaginable coming true for one young man and then for his tribe. It is more than the unimaginable coming true; it is a miracle.

So you may understand the extreme unimaginable events in this story let me give you a little history of the *Paradhi* tribes.

The *Paradhi* history shows that their ancestors were either forest inhabitants or wandering tribes who had distinct cultural identities. Up to the Mughal period the forests on which these communities were dependent were so vast, so remote, and so inaccessible that these areas yielded little or no income to the state treasuries. This situation changed with the advent of the East India Company. More and more forests were brought under its control for commercial exploitation. With their lives thus threatened, many from these *Paradhi* communities took to rebellion against the foreigners. In fact, many from these communities had taken part in and been martyred in the first war of independence against the British in 1857. That rebellion is still prevalent in today's communities.

The criminal branding of the tribe goes back to 1871 after the British passed the "Criminal Tribes Act." About a hundred and fifty tribes were branded as criminal, and the police were given sweeping powers to arrest them and watch over their movements. In 1952, the tribe was denotified as "criminal" and named as a nomadic tribe. However, this has not changed the public perception of the tribe, and they continue to be stigmatized and live as outcasts, further aggravating their backwardness and economic hardships.[1]

Even though the *Paradhis* do not allow outsiders, even the police, into their villages, it is actually a status symbol to have many criminal cases brought against them. A man would therefore have a better marriage prospect. In a country where over a quarter of parliamentarians face criminal charges, this is not as surprising as it might seem.

Paradhi poachers, for example, are one of the biggest threats to India's dwindling population of tigers, which they alone have eradicated from several national parks.

Their culture and civilization is changing fast with the changing times. Their traditional apparel used to be a "*pheta*" (headdress) and "l*angoti*" (loincloth) only. But things are now changing, as Western clothing for men is the norm.

For *Paradhis* there is little hope that they will **ever** be seen as ordinary Indians.[2]

But, in this unimaginable true story, you will see that there is hope for a better future.

In a world of instant gratification, we have totally forgotten the "Law of the Harvest" in our approach to ministry, especially in India. This story tells of seeding . . . years . . . watering . . . more years . . . then harvesting.

Contents

They Call Me Sir

Chapter 1:
Vasentha, a Bird-Catcher Boy

Aroused from a deep and peaceful sleep, Vasentha looked around the crammed shanty *zhopadi* wondering what had awakened him. As the fog lifted from his overtired senses, he realized it was the sound of a steady, pounding *paus* hammering on the corrugated tin sheeting thrown on top of the thatched roof of his cow-dung-and-brick *zhopadi*.

Could that be *paus*? This was June, and it never rained in June. He wished now that he hadn't wasted time covering the hole in the roof with the scavenged sheet of tin. This rhythmic drip-drip was a noise more annoying than the *pani* dripping in a metal *bharnu*. The lice in his hair had also been annoying, so his sleep had been minimal. When he yawned and stretched out his arms, he accidently struck Nanda. He hoped he hadn't disturbed his little sister's much-needed sleep.

Glancing over at his younger sisters, he knew they would not be able to fetch the wood needed for preparing the family's one meager meal. His drunken father certainly wouldn't be able to navigate the long trek into the jungle. So with resolve beyond his eight years, Vasentha arose from his paltry pallet-bed lying on the cow-dung floor.

Reaching for the only pair of pants he owned, he slowly pulled the hole-riddled fabric over his dirty, naked body. Knowing the gurgling of his empty stomach would not be pacified until he obtained wood for the cooking fire, he quietly stepped over the eight sleeping bodies of his family and crept toward the door. Gently pulling back the threadbare cloth, he slipped through the door opening. Sheets of water, wave after wave of driving rain, assaulted his young body. The warm *paus* revived him from the remaining drowsiness.

According to *Paradhi* history, Vasentha's ancestors were either forest inhabitants or wandering tribes that had distinct cultural identities. This heritage meant he was to be a hunter, definitely not a wood-gatherer, but who else in his family of nine was able to walk the more than fifteen kilometers to obtain enough wood for the daily needs of the family?

The beginning of a very early monsoon season meant this long, hot, and muddy daily trek would last for at least several weeks. Monsoon was not another word for *paus*. It was a season. This summer's monsoon had been preceded by a working-up-a-thirst drought so that when the waters came, they were drunk with relish. This also meant that the trek to find water for drinking had been alleviated for a short while.

As the steam rose in suffocating clouds, his mind was alert, but still there were dreams of a better life roaming within his limited intellect.

After leaving the muddy road and walking into the jungle, with its swaying, razor-like green weeds, water droplets beading on their slender stalks, intermixed with the flaming colors of the "farmer's devil weed," *lantana*, he let his artist's mind absorb the profusion of color and the little nuances of his environment. He was appreciative of time to dream; still, he must be vigilant, as the track might become a turbid stream.

Thankfully, it only took a little over an hour to find several large pieces of dry, gnarled tree limbs hidden under larger trees. Without too much tugging, he was able to loosen chunks from their perches and tie each fragment together with a handmade hemp cord. Wishing he had remembered to bring the piece of twisted, tattered cloth he could have used as a cushioning ring for his head, slowly he reached down and situated the bundle atop his head. This load would bring much pain to his scalp before he reached his isolated bird-catcher village. Sluggishly, he plodded down the already dreadfully muddy road.

The scorching hot June monsoon weather soon brought rivulets of sweat out to combine with the raindrops streaming down his face and back. Even with the rain, there was no washing away the annoying dirt-laden sweat.

Grumbling, he thought, *Why am I doing such a thing? Maybe my sisters are old enough to carry this load of sticks.* He waited beside the road as a herd of cattle that ruled the roads passed. The cows roamed freely, arrogantly, secure in the centuries-old instinct that they were sacred and inviolable.

Not only was the steaming heat of the road hurting his bare feet as his legs became more covered with mud, but his legs also began to itch. *If only dry weather would come,* he thought, *then this trek would be easier. Well, then again, maybe not. The dust would be just as troublesome.* The sizeable sticks on his head were getting appallingly heavy, so again he shifted his burdensome load.

"This is women's work," he lamented.

Again, he wondered, *Why am I doing such a thing? I long for the day my sisters or even my brother is old enough to carry this burden of sticks. I want time to paint on the wall of our* zhopadi. *I stole some unused, beautiful, sky-blue house paint from a hut in a nearby Muslim village. I could "find" some more and make a picture that keeps drifting around in my brain. This paint color will be such a nice, perfect color for the summer sky.*

My mother works exceptionally hard cleaning other women's pots, but still the wage she earns is not enough rupees *to feed our family. Someday, yes, someday, I will not be hungry. If only my father did not use the meager amount of* rupees *we earn on alcohol,* he bemoaned.

Every day the walk to the jungle area got longer . . . nearly fifteen kilometers now. The once-lush vegetation of a verdant paradise was disappearing and there was no longer wood left nearby with which to make a fire for cooking.

I could walk very fast, he thought. *However, at this pace, it will take most of my day.* His *Paradhi* tribe was nomadic, but he had no desire to move again. Once they were great hunters and had the technique of catching the *titur,* a small quail-like bird down to an art form.

I need to rest and get out of the blasted paus, thought Vasentha. *I have a tongue-hanging-out thirst.*

With this thought, he realized he was quickly approaching the banyan tree with its many-fingered roots reaching the ground, making a perfect umbrella, the only possible protection from the rain.

He smiled as he decided; *I will stop and rest when I get to this place.*

Chapter 2:
Lone Tree

Aroused from the mist of sleepy consciousness by the pounding *paus,* Dr. Suresh Wanhkede found it very difficult to slide off his cool, comfortable communal bed he shared with his wife, Nupi, and two daughters, Shini and Rachael. He would miss the day when the girls would be old enough to sleep in their own beds, already prepared in the newly decorated second bedroom. Tenderly, he leaned over and carefully kissed each sleeping child on her soft, warm cheek.

As he dressed in his most rain-resistant clothing, he muttered, "Why do I go to villages on such a very rainy day? I do not really have important reason." He argued with himself as he slipped into his black trousers and bright-blue T-shirt, "Well, other than the lost souls of the needy farmers."

The moment he stepped out of the unassuming brick-and-concrete house, he discerned a feeling of unusualness about the morning. His spirit was convicted of his previous thoughts and mutterings; he slithered into his frayed green windbreaker. Uncovering the Hero Honda 100 and stuffing his belongings into the *dickey* (a side pocket), he threw his legs over the tank and began riding the motorcycle down the potholed, muddy road in front of his humble home.

Even at this early hour, motorcycles and scooters clogged the road like flies on dead meat. Horns blared; shouts of noisy street vendors and roars of lorries assailed the doctor's sensibilities.

But still the unsolicited thoughts came. *Did God really call me to practice my veterinarian medicine in these far-away villages? I am doing God's work. Why is he not providing good raincoat for me?*

Do I really make a difference to these farmers, he ponders? Well, yesterday I did deliver a calf. The cow had been near death during the birthing process. The farmer was desperate to not lose his only means of income. Now he had a new calf also. This thought made the doctor very joyful. While working with the farmer to save the cow and her calf, he was able to talk to the farmer about the love of *Yeshu*.

Yes, first and foremost, this is exactly why God wants me to be a veterinarian. There is true satisfaction in being skilled to help these extremely poor and marginalized village people.

Without the help of people from Prakash for India[3], I would be in the same circumstances as these poor farmers. I will not forget that I am just a poor village boy too. They gave me the ray of hope for a better life by helping me get my veterinarian doctorate degree.

Prakash for India schools provide training with a Christian emphasize so many disadvantaged young Indians can learn a viable trade and have a better life.

There were times in my village when I was beaten for having dreams of being a doctor. I was thought to be arrogant. "No poor village boy can be a doctor," the gang of boys would taunt.

After hours of fighting the traffic and enduring the pounding *paus*, Dr. Suresh thought, *This day is so demanding. I need to stop, rest, and drink some water.* Just then, he saw a banyan tree with branches that sent out a multitude of adventitious roots, causing it to spread over a large area in the perfect umbrella shape . . . the only lone tree in the vicinity. The tree formed a roof of leafy shadows and protection.

What a good place for resting and shelter from the now-hammering paus, he reasoned, thinking, *Nupi always tells me to drink more water. What a good place for resting.* So he hauled his motorbike over to the tree for its partial protection from the *paus* and removed his filtered bottled water from the *dickey*.

Just then, Vasentha approached the tree, only to find a man on a motorcycle drinking water on the only protected spot. Oh, how good a drink of *pani* would taste just now! He would also love to see the motorcycle up close, but he was much too frightened to get close to the well-dressed *Marathi* Indian.

I am a tribal and I know he would not share his pani *and the protection of the tree with me. The gods have made my fate,* he grieved. The *Paradhi* tribe often faced harassment by Indian law-enforcement agencies and disdain from the Indian population.

What have I done? Is he a policeman? He does not wear a uniform, but that does not make a difference. All outsiders think we are robbers since the British deemed us the "criminal tribe" years ago, Vasentha thought.

Is he laughing inside because I am a boy carrying firewood? Does he know I am from the violent Paradhi *tribe?*

So disheartened, Vasentha slowly trudged on.

The man intently watched the woebegone adolescent boy with bones sharply defined beneath his dark skin.

Something in the doctor's heart stirred for this pitiful young boy. It brought back many memories of his paltry village childhood. *I, too, at one time in my life, moved through the same conditions. But for Prakash for India, I would still be in the misery of village India.*

The doctor's heart ached for the painfully thin, dirty, grime-encrusted young boy.

He is so filthy and so thin from lack of good, healthy food, not unlike many children I see in the numerous villages I visit. At least my father was a farmer, and growing up . . . until the hostel years . . . I had nearly enough to eat as a child, even if I did take many beatings from the villagers for my dream of becoming a doctor, Dr. Suresh reminisced.

Why has this boy caught my attention? I know he must be from the rock-crusher village or maybe even the tribal bird-catcher village. But, oh, that is so far away, he couldn't have possibly walked that far in this downpour, the doctor rationalized.

The landscape around the bird-catcher village is somewhat like a picture of the desolate moon surface—dry, desolate in summer with scummy water pools resting in the bottom of large, excavated manmade craters. The mud-brick *zhopadi* huts are scattered far apart—not the normal village of concentrated habitation.

He sadly watched the young boy, walking with the distinctive *Paradhi* sneaking gait, slog down the busy road.

Chapter 3:
Dr. Suresh and Boy

When Dr. Suresh returned that evening to his home, with its peaceful, pale-green mosaic tile floors gleaming from their daily scrubbing, he told his wife about seeing the young boy on the road that day.

"Did you follow him?" she asked. "How can you ever help him if you do not know where he lives? And, Suresh, my dear husband, you cannot help every young boy you see along the road. Also, aren't they the nomadic tribe that is known for their violence?"

The tugging in the doctor's heart simply wouldn't go away. Immediately after a dinner of chicken curry, rice, and *chapthis*, he lay on his *diwan* recollecting the day's incidents. The image of this boy churned up within him. For hours, sleep eluded him. Quietly, he later slipped out of the communal bed, hoping not to disturb his sleeping family. He knelt and prayed, "Lord, I have such a burden for this boy. If this is a person I am supposed to lend a hand to, then show me where he lives."

For about two weeks, Dr. Suresh continued to struggle. He wanted to expunge the boy from his memory. Knowing the caste system of India means that *Paradhis* are not allowed to attend school or own land. They die beside the road and no one cares or will help them in any way. Most villages have no running water, even though the government is trying to get a well drilled in every village in India, the *Paradhis* are at the bottom of the list The *Paradhis* suffer from extremely poor health.

Finally, giving up on resisting the still, small voice of God, Dr. Suresh walked out of his home into the unpromising morning, unaware of the smell of the honeysuckle vine encasing his front veranda door or the beauty of the sparkling water droplets hanging on each verdant leaf. Grudgingly, he dressed for the dismal weather and rode his motorcycle back to the same banyan tree where he had previously encountered the young boy . . . and waited. Figuring that the boy had a daily routine, he hoped to not have a prolonged stay sitting under the large tree.

"Lord, you know this is so not —or, one bit— anything I ever wanted to do."

For three days, he carried out this same routine. Sitting under the tree for periods of time reinforced Dr. Suresh's feelings of this not being something he wanted to do.

On the third day, just as he was about to give up and return home, down the road trudged the skinny boy hauling another gigantic load of firewood on his head. He looked even more painfully thin, his bones more sharply defined beneath his dark, dirty skin.

"Hey, you, boy," says Dr. Suresh. "*Aajao*, come here and rest with me. The tree will give us protection from the *paus*."

Stunned, then looking around to make sure, Vasentha could not believe his eyes or his ears. *This* Marathi *Indian was actually speaking to him. Was this the same man who was sitting in his favorite spot under the tree a few weeks back?*

The boy only stopped and stared, but not one muscle would move toward the protection of the tree.

Speaking slowly and using his hands, Dr. Suresh began to speak. "I am Dr. Suresh, and I saw you walking here before. Are you from a village nearby?"

Vasentha was so scared he was unable to find his speech, even if he could have spoken *Marathi* proficiently. His tribal language was completely dissimilar. Thousands of thoughts came rushing through his head.

Why did this doctor want to talk with him? *This man could hurt me or steal firewood, but he has kind face and he is very clean and he has shoes. He has no police uniform. He will not do me harm,* he concluded. *What could he want with me, a poor tribal boy?*

Timidly, Vasentha began to speak. "Sir," he began in his broken *Marathi*, "I live in bird-catcher village. It quite far away, but I walk road every day to jungle, gather firewood for family."

The language was a tribal mixture and very different from the *Marathi* common to the area. But, again with sign language and a God-given understanding, Dr. Suresh asked, "Would you like to ride with me on my motorcycle to the *Chai* Stall just down the road?"

Chapter 4:
Chai Stall

*C*hai, *a word any boy would understand . . .
and a motorcycle ride all in one day. The gods
must be happy today,* rejoiced Vasentha.
He had passed the *Chai* Stall every day, but never
in his wildest imagination dreamed it would be a
place he could stop and buy the hot tea, milk, and
spice mixture. *They will never serve me*, he thought
despondently.

Carrying the load of sticks across his lap while
sitting on the back of the black-and-silver motorcycle
proved to be a bigger challenge than Vasentha
thought it would be. But no amount of effort would
deter him from experiencing this magnificent
encounter. He could just imagine what his sisters and
brother would think when he told his tale around the
communal fire tonight.

The *Chai* Stall, constructed of only a few *saboble*
poles tied together with stripped bamboo, had a
thatched roof of dried weeds and a ragged blue
plastic tarp thrown over one area to give some shelter

from the *paus*. There was a noticeable hesitation by the *chai* peddler to serve the grimy boy, but after one look from Dr. Suresh, he began to stir the pot of *chai*.

Watching the snaggle-toothed vendor serve the steaming tea concoction in small silver-colored metal cups, Vasentha thought he would never again have such a magnificent experience. *Masala chai,* with all the sugar and cream he wanted, was a luxury of tremendous proportions.

Someday, I will have all the sugar I want. I will buy MY sugar. It will be MY sugar!

Dr. Suresh asked me many questions, but I didn't understand everything he said, he thought. *His language is very different from mine. We just sat and looked out through a curtain of* paus *at all the passing lorries, bullock carts, motorcycles, and throngs of people, the* paus *not seeming to hamper the activities of the daily routine. I would answer,* "HO," *a yes answer to the many questions, even when I did not understand all that the doctor had said.*

He asked why I wasn't in school. I told him I did have my name registered as being in second standard because a big politician had come around to village last year and put all the village children on list. But I had never attended school. The politician didn't care about me. He only wanted to show the numbers so everyone would think he was doing his job. Also, I didn't have proper clothes or beautiful book bag like all the children from other villages who attended school. No Paradhi *child had* ever *attended school.*

With immense effort, I was able to convey to him that I wanted to be an artist and liked to draw. Furthermore, I wanted to become a leader in my village. This dream was so colossal that it seemed unattainable and unimaginable. It is very unusual for a village boy to even think about the future or have dreams.

Dr. Suresh was intrigued. *I was amazed at how much information he was able to extract from me. Normally, I was a very quiet person, left to dream in my own little world.*

All too soon, the teatime came to an end.

The late afternoon was hot and a film of steam rose from the mud. As the motorcycle negotiated the deeply rutted path—the ruts were flooded with water, and low swarms of flies and gnats settled into little clouds above the mud—they entered the rambling and battered mishmash of run-down *zhopadis* and shacks.

It was an exciting trip back into the village for the young boy, as all the elders saw him riding on a motorcycle with the doctor. The *paus* in their faces seemed to no longer be an irritant.

A few dung-fueled fires were burning under the shelter of the lean-to. Odors, filth, and disease infested this village. Ragged children with flies covering their sores watched with amazement as the motorcycle travelled through the village.

Dropping the stack of wood as soon as they came to a stop, Vasentha shouted, "*Maa, maa!*" and excitedly introduced his mother to the doctor, but his father was too drunk to get up off the floor of the *zhopadi*. Besides, he was embarrassingly naked.

Savoring the adventure and trying to embed it in his memory, Vasentha was unaware of his growling stomach. Because he had been so long in returning with the load of wood, there would be no meal anytime soon. *Well, it is not so bad; I had sugar today.*

I wondered if the doctor recognized my village as very unusual.

There were eighteen crumbling, decrepit mud–brick hovels with open drains and leaking roofs of thatch, sticks, rusted corrugated iron, and miscellaneous debris. The debris was made of old lorries' tires and rocks. Instead of being sandwiched close together, the *zhopadis* were spread out over a four-acre area of desolate wasteland. Vasentha's home sat by the single-track path winding across to the one lonely tree surrounded by a few sprigs of grass. The only water came from the run-off rainwater that stagnated to a thick green layer of filth in the granite pits left from the rock-crushers' devastation— but it was his home.

As the doctor rode away, the motorcycle tires causing small specks of mud to fly through the sodden air, I remembered I had not thanked him. "Dhanyawad," *I yelled, as I waved excitedly.*

Chapter 5:
Doctor Returns

For the following days, as Vasentha plodded down the now-dusty road, leaving a small cloud of swirling powder, eyes roaming the roadside, he anxiously looked to see if the doctor had returned to the spot under the tree.

After what he felt to be an eternity, the doctor unexpectedly arrived in the village unchanged for centuries with his wife and two daughters. As the cloud of dust announced the arrival of the marvelous black-and-silver motorcycle traveling directly up to his *zhopadi*, Vasentha's chest filled with pride. Just as he thought it could not be any more wonderful, they brought out gifts of drawing materials and kerosene for the small *primus* burner they used for light at night. *My* maa *stood in awe with her tattered sari pulled over her straggly, dirt-encrusted long hair.* By then there was the typical throng of children jabbering in their tribal language, giggling in the universal language of kids, all vying for a look-see.

Due to his interest in all things *village*, Dr. Suresh asked to see how the village made its income for its meager survival. Luckily, Vasentha's dark-skinned father with the spindly limbs of the underfed was sober enough to show by his gestures and expressions

how he used the crudely woven, rectangular, large box-like hemp nets and leather shield to hunt and catch birds in the jungle. Carefully and with precision, he laid the odd-shaped netting on the ground. Then, with the flair of an artist, he arranged a line of grain positioned to lead to the gap in the end of the netting. Next, with the stature of a warrior and the dark, leathery skin of a village dweller, he crouched behind the shield as if lying in wait for birds to unknowingly enter the trap. The mini program ended with a simple bow.

The government, in an effort to curb the poaching of tigers, had made a law against the hunting and killing of *any* wild animal in India. So now it was illegal for Vasentha's village menfolk to hunt. How were they going to eat? Every day, they used to be able to ensnare a horde of small *titur,* quail-like birds and sell them in the marketplace in trade for staple foods and kerosene. Now there was no legal means to make money. Therefore, they had resorted to making an illegal form of wine.

"... People from time immemorial have been pursuing the caste system that defined job -positions: weaving, carpentry, hunting, and as such are hereditary jobs. So there must have been hereditary criminals also who pursued their forefathers' professions."[4]

All too soon the doctor's visit ended, but not without a promise of his return. Even the head gave his unequivocal consent. This time Vasentha remembered to say a truly grateful "*Dhanyawad*" before the doctor and family left. He could not wait to examine the gifts of drawing materials and lose himself in artistic pursuits.

Chapter 6:
Bath and Haircut

In Vasentha's village, not unlike many villages in India, there are many nights when the only source of light is the moon and glistening stars above. Most of these nights are used for storytelling. Since the village has no written language, this is the only way for the younger village members to learn about the historic four-thousand-year legacy. The colorful stories are excitingly told, with unusual symbols and gestures making the history sound thrilling.

As an eight-year-old, Vasentha thought, *I do not remember when we moved to this place. I do know we are considered nomads and squatters. Since we have stripped this land of all its foliage, I wonder if we will have to move again. I am hoping not.*

Now that the monsoon season was over, the big holes blasted in the ground by the rock crushers had filled with water. This made the daily trek to get water much shorter. In about another week, the water would begin to taste bad because the surface would be covered with a green scum. *I really do not know*

this name "scum," but that is what I hear it being called,
Vasentha mused.

Dr. Suresh was in constant communication with
the executive director of Prakash for India and his
wife. In fact, he felt they were his American parents,
calling them Papi and Nani. Soon after his first visit
with his family to Vasentha's village, the doctor
expressed in an email, "Nani, I know that God has
called me to work with these *Paradhi* villagers. But
they STINK! How can I continue to work with them?"

Quickly returning his email, Nani said, "Maybe
God wants you to teach them hygiene before you try
to teach them about Jesus."

The next morning, as Dr. Suresh was rummaging
through all the bathroom cupboards and supplies,
Nupi asked, "Suresh, what on earth are you doing?"

"Well," Nani wrote that I needed to teach
Vasentha's village hygiene. I'm trying to find some
scissors, shampoo, soap, a comb, and an extra
toothbrush."

"For sure this is not what they taught you in
veterinary college," she giggled.

With his brow creased with worry, he told
himself he was a doctor and his compassion and
desire for transformation was natural, animal or
human. He would just pack the supplies in his
motorcycle's *dickey* and wait for the right time to

start teaching cleanliness . . . a totally unimaginable concept to this tribe.

Amidst the swirl of dust as Dr. Suresh's motorcycle made its way across the dirt track from the main road, he regularly returned to Vasentha's village. He even told the villagers they needed to take baths and brush their teeth. No one in the village had ever done these things. *Are these good things?* they wondered. Vasentha determined to do anything the doctor said. After all, he was a doctor. At this time, Vasentha didn't know the good doctor was an animal doctor.

Gathering his blue-striped cloth bag of supplies out of the *dickey*, Dr. Suresh tried to sound like the most thrilling event in the world was about to take place. All the ragtag children gathered around him expectantly.

Dr. Suresh said enticingly, "Let's all go down to that pool of water over there. I am going to teach you some new and exciting things."

Step by step, the children cautiously maneuvered down the small rocky path. A niggling of fear fluttered in Vasentha's belly about *new* things. Tribals are never too excited about change.

First the doctor brought out a shiny pair of what he called scissors. He said that he wanted to cut all of the children's hair. Fear ascended from Vasentha's belly to his throat as the doctor said, "Vasentha, why not let us start with you?" The sweat of fear broke out on his forehead, but he could deny the doctor nothing. *Would this be painful?* No one in the tribe had ever cut his or her hair.

Slowly, looking from side to side, Vasentha arose and took a seat on a rock in front of the doctor. Carefully taking a handful of hair, the doctor cut—no pain—and Vasentha smiled. All the other kids sniggered. The doctor gently continued around Vasentha's bent head until all the long, snarled, bug-infested hair was lying in a heap on the ground. Vasentha thought, *It feels freeing to no longer have the matted hair on the back of my neck.* Now the other children rushed forward. Once again, Dr. Suresh had to command order, not a trait inborn in tribals. Sitting the remaining children in rows, he said, "Vasentha, bring *ek* by *ek* each child to me. You will be in charge."

Vasentha's chest puffed out as he motioned for a new inductee to take a turn for the unique experience of a haircut. This was the beginning of Vasentha's working relationship with Dr. Suresh.

Just when everyone thought the ordeal was over, the doctor bent over and again rummaged through his striped cloth bag, bringing out a white bar of something called *sabun*, and said, "Now I will teach you how to bathe and wash your hair."

Oh dear, what now?

"*Aajao*, please come," said the doctor, "let us go into the water."

Glad for his short pants, Vasentha watched the doctor gingerly push back the thick layer of green scum as he entered the water; he encouraged all to follow. Then he began to demonstrate how to wash. Suddenly, with a whoop and a holler, all fear was gone in the chaos of splashing and squealing. *Sabun* bubbles mixed with green froth. The filth of the water did not deter the children from an exuberant first bath.

Dr. Suresh stressed that all the children should continue this bathing routine once a week. Faithfully, Vasentha adhered to the cleansing routine. He even tried to get his brother, four sisters, and a recently adopted cousin to do the same thing, but they saw no reason for what was considered extra work.

Chapter 7:
School . . . Unimaginable

After months of dropping by and building stronger relationships, Dr. Suresh knew first and foremost he would have to obtain the approval of the elders of the village if Vasentha was ever going to be able to go to school.

School? Was it just an unimaginable, wishful notion?

The questions bombarded the doctor. No one in the history of the village or even the entire tribe had ever attended school. In fact, their language had never been written. It was only tonal and verbal. Who would do the work if the children were in school?

Vasentha was in second standard on paper, but had never attended. The school lessons were taught

in *Marathi*. Why would Vasentha need to learn such things? But the doctor persisted. He had seen astuteness and creative distinctiveness in the drawings that were painted all over Vasentha's *zhopadi* and on the paper tablet he had brought to Vasentha not long after their first meeting. He had a sudden thought: *How had this young boy managed to get paint anyway?* There was intelligence in those large brown eyes that needed stimulation. The doctor needed a way of unlocking Vasentha's ultimate potential.

The tribal elders questioned why the doctor was interested in them.

"Because I once was a very poor boy and I received help. I am concerned and want to help Vasentha. I want to do for one, what I wish I could do for all."

The doctor's arguments were very compelling; especially when he told the elders he and his wife would pay all the fees and uniform expenses. He had not yet okayed this new expenditure with his wife, but . . . well . . . God would surely provide. It was amazing what a little positive input, guidance, and love could do.

During dinner that evening, Suresh sheepishly said, "Nupi, what do you think, errr . . . well, how about we take Vasentha on as a family project? Well, actually, I really have already committed to the elders that we would pay for his uniforms and books if they would allow him to attend school. Soooo, dear, sweet lady, what do you think?"

In unison the two girls jumped up and yelled, "*Ho! Ho!* It would be fun to help." Nupi simply shrugged her shoulders. He was blown away by their enthusiastic *yes* response, yet why should he be? Their family had thoroughly enjoyed each visit to the village and prayed fervently for its people.

Chapter 8:
Miracle of School

Streaks of orange and pink splashed the morning sky in a welcoming design as Dr. Suresh walked out to greet the new day.

There was a flurry of activity as he picked up Vasentha for yet another motorcycle journey, not even sure if he could get Vasentha into school because none of the required preregistration had taken place. Together they headed to the *Kalmeshwar* School. With a quick prayer, trying to ignore the anxious quivering in his stomach, Dr. Suresh entered the school office. Vasentha shyly followed behind. Thinking he would need to advocate his case, the doctor was in utter shock when the headmaster said, "This is miracle thing, because there is only one seat left in the second standard and it is for Vasentha's caste."

The government of India set the regulation and number of seats available for each caste. Even though the law said no student from the *Paradhi* tribe could attend school, there was still an allocation for a student.

The caste system was officially outlawed in 1950, but it still dominated the social structure and behavior everywhere in India.

After officially registering by filling out a mountain of paperwork and obtaining the book list, man and boy, riding the Hero Honda 100, wove in and out of traffic, becoming a part of the surging wave. There was no mercy shown to those who didn't ride it; you had to join in or get swatted aside very quickly. The lorries hogged the middle of the road and belched out palls of dense, sooty exhaust fumes. Unwaveringly, they forged on to Nagpur[5], the big city. At stoplights they squeezed into the front of the pack like all the other motorcycles.

Besides the necessary shopping, Vasentha needed to be measured for uniforms. Then they were off to the bookstore, where the shopkeeper (his gums and teeth stained red from chewing *betel nut*, a speck of red foam appearing at the corner of his mouth) sat intrigued as doctor and boy gathered all the books on the book list. They bought books, paper, pencils, crayons, and a blue-striped book bag. Never in his

young life had Vasentha received so much attention. Even though he was scared to death by the ride into town, it was once more an extremely exciting day in his young life.

Again the doctor stressed that Vasentha would have to bathe and brush his teeth every day . . . *WHAT?* But he did want to go to school. The next day, the doctor also brought a hairbrush and some good-tasting white paste in a tube for brushing teeth. *What is wrong with the ashes of cow-dung on my finger that I have always used?* wondered Vasentha. *Well, actually, only once in a very great while.*

Vasentha practiced how Dr. Suresh had shown him to fold his uniforms at night so they would look presentable for wearing the next day. Each sleeve of the white shirt was to be folded neatly in, and then it was folded in half. The tan short pants were to be folded and laid under the shirt. There was a blue-and-red striped tie, which remained tied and simply slipped over Vasentha's head. He had never even had clothes before, just one pair of tattered, threadbare hand-me-down shorts. Now he had two uniforms and undershorts for daytime. *Being civilized is a lot of work and effort,* thought Vasentha.

The first day of school . . . *I have on no occasion been so intimidated in my short life*, thought Vasentha. The noise of all the other children running and laughing was overwhelming. He was bigger than the current students in his class. All of them had gone to school since they were very young. Vasentha was eight running (all Indians and tribals are either running to a year number or complete. The younger they are the more it is running) and tall for his age, so they put him in the second standard even though this was the first day for him to ever attend school.

Clinging to his new, blue-striped book bag, he slowly walked into the schoolroom, heading directly to the back, nearly stumbling over one boy as he gazed at the breathtaking pictures that covered the bright-green walls of the classroom. Hesitantly, he sat on the patterned rug covering the hard concrete floor. The sun was glistening through the smudged windows and the fan overhead made a "whirring" sound. He sat mesmerized and stared at all the activity around him. There were many things he had never seen or heard before. Even understanding the teacher took all of his attention. *I must do well for Dr. Suresh*, he reminded himself. It was hard to concentrate; the books had so many brilliant and colorful pictures that he wanted to draw instead of learning to read the words. This was an astonishing new world he never even knew existed.

Vasentha did everything with one-hundred percent effort. So because he had worked diligently for excellent grades in school, Dr. Suresh rewarded Vasentha with a small metal suitcase that contained more colored pencils, a large drawing tablet, and some watercolor paints with brushes. Again, this was beyond anything he had ever dreamt of.

Chapter 9:
Foreign Guests

A huge, swirling cloud of dust was on the trail, catching the attention of the villagers. The white official-looking vehicle was zigzagging on the track, trying to miss the large ruts and potholes. When the large white Armada stopped, out stepped a *Gora Saheb*. There was instant fear, until Dr. Suresh jumped out and yelled his greeting, "*Nameste.*" Womenfolk nudged one another and whispered behind their hands. The naked children swarmed, arms crossed over their chests, gazing with solemn, round black eyes. At seeing Dr. Suresh, Vasentha, in his typical slow gait and arms akimbo, came forward with the new hug greeting. Everyone then huddled around, squatting down in typical Indian fashion, to see why the *Gora Saheb* and the white *memsaheb* (with never-before-seen golden hair and blue eyes) had come. As they talked in yet another language, Vasentha finally realized they had come to see his artwork.

The crowd grew and jostled for the best viewing positions of the *Gora Saheb. Why is he so interested?* thought Vasentha. Timidly, he retrieved the small metal case and set it on the dusty ground beside the *Gora Saheb*. Running to the tiny mud-brick *zhopadi*, Vasentha's *maa* brought out their very best blanket for the honored man to sit on . . . not caring that it was jumping with lice. The man looked at the blanket and thought, *What would Jesus do?* So down he sat, and viewed all of Vasentha's amazing artistic work. Vasentha seated himself in the typical hunched squat all Indians used.

The children stood around every edge of the blanket with toes wiggling in the dirt. Only the reprimands of Vasentha kept them from hovering over the *Gora Saheb*. A certain flyblown air reeked from the unwashed bodies. The god-lady stood back. She certainly had to be a god with such a light skin tone and yellow hair. The villagers were unaware there were any humans in the world with such skin or eye color. This captivated Vasentha's artist's heart. Later he would call this white woman Nani.

Vasentha could not believe his good luck when the *Gora Saheb* offered him 100 *rupees* for his drawing of a *wagh* (tiger). The gods must be contented this day. Later, Dr. Suresh told him that the *wagh* picture was to be used in letters sent to many Americans telling of the ministries of Prakash for India.

Chapter 10: Storytelling and Honesty

After two years of school, the elders decided that this was a good thing and allowed two girls from the village to start attending. These girls, so embedded in poverty and abuse that their lives were seemingly hopeless, were for the first time given a ray of hope.

As Vasentha learned to read, he would practice by reading Bible stories around the fire at night. With the lamp flickering, Vasentha would tell the stories from Scripture with countless facial expressions. He would use the precious kerosene lamp for light, but all the villagers enjoyed the stories too much to care about the expense.

Dr. Suresh had given him a *Marathi* Bible, so he read in *Marathi* and spoke in his native tongue. It never occurred to him that he was doing a very difficult thing.

One day the *Gora Saheb,* now considered Papi, came again to the village with a foreign visitor. After hugging Vasentha—the new traditional greeting—the visitors looked in and out of the decrepit *zhopadi,* taking photos with a large and very fancy black camera. The guests were very interested in Vasentha's artwork. After they left, Vasentha saw the foreign visitor's camera on the ground. Knowing that it had great value and his tribe could sell it for many *rupees,* Vasentha stood guard—scared even to touch it—for many hours until Dr. Suresh returned. Vasentha did not want his newfound honor to be spoiled by his thieving tribe.

Chapter 11:
The Pot

With permission from the village elders, Dr. Suresh and his family started a Children's Club program for all the village children. The youngsters were so excited to learn to sing action songs at their own rhythm and to hear fascinating stories. There were even brightly colored crayons and construction paper for them to use—things these kids had never even seen, let alone were able to use.

Dr. Suresh and his family began developing a relationship of *Yeshu's* love with these children and their families.

After a few months' work, a special performance was prepared for some American visitors. The youngsters all worked feverishly to make props. They gathered random bricks to make a brick well. A potter's wheel was made from an old wagon wheel. Not-so-skillfully applied paint on cardboard cutouts, in the shape of pots supplied by Nupi, added to their array of props. Much time was taken to gather rocks to designate a path from the potter's wheel to the well.

Finding flowers was another feat. It took a very long walk to find any wildflowers growing. The children cared for them very carefully until the program started. They felt the flowers were probably the most valuable things they had ever possessed.

Practice, practice, practice for the appointed day.

The excitement for the program to start was electric. The children borrowed chairs, hoping these white-skinned people would be comfortable. The children worried. *Will they like our program? It will be so hard to concentrate on our parts with these very different and interesting people sitting there.*

Dr. Suresh cut all the youngsters' hair that morning. Vasentha wondered, *Why do these white people not like long hair?* All the children even had to go down in the rock-crater pond and grudgingly bathe.

The visitors arrived in a flurry of dust. Greetings were given, chairs occupied. Finally the anticipated program began. There was laughter from the guests as singing of the action songs started. On no occasion before had the children sung together, so everyone was on his or her own beat and note. Still, at the end, a thunderous applause noted approval.

Then the drama commenced. Each child acted out his or her part and Nupi read the story. Each child would carry this badge of honor for life, identifying

themselves as "The Pot" or "The Flower Girl."
Vasentha was "The Potter."

"In a village there lived a potter who made pots of mud. He made big pots, small pots, and all kinds of

pots. He worked very hard from morning to evening. But he had one problem. He had to fetch water from a far-away place. Every day he took two pots tied to the ends of a large wooden stick over his shoulders and brought water for his work. He did this for days, months, and years. Every day the pots carried water for him. One of the pots was very happy, while the other pot was sad. The sad pot had a crack in it and, therefore, would be half empty by the time they reached home. The good pot always mocked the cracked one and said, 'I am more useful to the master than you. I bring the water full and you bring only half of the water.'

One day the cracked pot said to his master, 'Master, I am of no use to you. Please throw me

away and get a new pot so you can bring a pot full of water for yourself.' But the master said to the pot, 'Dear pot, today as we go to get the water, I want you to look around and see what you can see.' The next day, the pot was more observant and noticed the roadside as they went and came back from the well. After they reached home, the master asked the cracked pot, 'What did you notice around you?' The pot said, 'I saw beautiful flowers along the road.' The master said, 'Those beautiful flowers are there all because of you.' The pot was surprised to hear this. He said, 'How can a cracked pot like me with no value do this?' The master said, 'I knew that you were cracked and, therefore, I wanted to use you as you were. I planted those flowering plants along the road on your side, so when we came back with the water, you were dripping and unknowingly watering these plants. And so don't degrade yourself; just be willing to serve me and remember that I will make the best use of you.'"

Nupi then said, "The teaching of this skit is that no matter how useless we may think we are, *Yeshu* knows our potential and uses us abundantly for his glory when we are willing to be available for him."

By the time the program had ended, about sixty people were sitting all around hearing about the love of *Yeshu*, and they didn't know they were in "church."

Chapter 12:
Second Miracle of School

"It's Tomorrow."

The most difficult occasion arrived when it was time for Vasentha to enter Seventh Standard. It meant that he would have to attend a school much farther away from his village. He was already walking five kilometers, and the other school was six times that far. The elders just couldn't see how it was possible. They did have a rusted red bicycle with flat, sagging wheels. The village women used it to haul bundles of firewood, but the rubber tires were flat and needed too much patch-up for them to afford repairs.

Dr. Suresh could not afford the extra expenses either, so he wrote to his Nani and Papi in the U.S. asking for help. Papi was now the executive director of Prakash for India, but years earlier, Dr. Suresh and his wife, Nupi, had had the phenomenal experience of going to the U.S. on a Prakash for India promotional mission conference trip. They had presented Prakash for India to multiple congregations and Dr. Suresh shared how Prakash for India had helped him get his doctorate of veterinary medicine. The couple had lived with Nani and Papi for three months and became their Indian kids. It was on this trip that the dream of Vet-Med Outreach[6] was verbalized. Vet-Med Outreach is veterinary help to poor farmers and programs of training so that young Indians can become self-reliant.

Nani had taught so many helpful household tips to the newly married couple, even buying extra underclothing, just so she did not have to wash every day.

She had told Nupi upon arrival that she would do all the washing in her beautiful, big white machine. One day Nani walked into the couples' allocated bathroom and saw their wet underclothing hanging over the towel rack. Immediately, she went to Nupi.

"Nupi, I told you I would wash your clothing. I'm not angry, but why are there wet undies in the bathroom?"

With a shameful bowed head, Nupi replied, "Nani, we only have one extra."

"Oh, my goodness! We have to go shopping."

Nani and Papi had not responded to Suresh's plea for help and Vasentha's new school was starting very soon. On faith, the doctor went to Nagpur and ordered uniforms for Vasentha. Where would he get the *rupees* if Nani and Papi did not help? God would provide, he simply believed.

On the Saturday before school was to start the following Monday, Dr. Suresh and his family were eating breakfast at the wooden table just off the kitchen. A surprising knock at the door had the whole family standing in anticipation of guests. They opened the door to be greeted by the weathered, lined-by-time face of Vasentha's uncle. With an embarrassed lowered head, the uncle said he came instead of Vasentha's mother because she felt it was shameful for her to request that Dr. Suresh help Vasentha to continue on in school. The uncle begged the doctor to find the *rupees* for Vasentha to go to school.

School had now become very important and prestigious to the village elders. Dr. Suresh said, "We do not have the *rupees* to provide any more than we are doing now. I don't know why, but I have had no word from America, so the only thing I know to do is pray. Will you get on your knees and pray with me?"

The uncle had never prayed before to this *Yeshu*, but if it would help, he was willing to do anything. The gods he knew were never kind and extremely threatening. His gods were in the trees and rocks and did not seem to hear his prayers, even though he went to their shrines with offerings each day.

Dr. Suresh began to pray, thanking *Yeshu* for his love and kindness to them. He also prayed that this uncle would come to know *Yeshu* as his personal Savior. Then he brought his petition before *Yeshu* for money to let Vasentha go to school on Monday. If Vasentha didn't join his class on Monday, he would have to wait for a full year before he could reapply.

"And *Yeshu*, bring us your answer *tomorrow*. Amen."

Back in America, Nani and Papi were just returning from a vacation and sitting in their home office going through sheaves of paperwork and mail when out of the blue Nani asked Papi, "Did you ever email Suresh and tell him we would help with Vasentha's expenses?"

"Oh, no, I forgot. I will call India tomorrow."

"But Papi, because of the time difference, tomorrow will be too late. It will be Monday morning in just a few hours. Call right now."

"But it will be four in the morning there," Papi argued.

Nani countered, "I don't think Suresh will care if he knows we are going to help Vasentha start school."

"Okay, okay."

Suresh could not understand why his phone was ringing at such an early hour. There must be an emergency.

When he heard Papi's voice, he began to cry. "Oh, Papi, it is *tomorrow*." He then began to tell the story of the uncle coming. Papi never got to tell him he was going to help. Suresh just knew why he had called.

"Nupi, wake up, wake up. Papi just called and I have to ride out to Vasentha's village and get him ready for school. Isn't God good? It's tomorrow. Help me find the uniforms we had made for Vasentha."

It was a long but wonderful early morning ride. Never had the night sky, with its deep blue-purple coloring, calling out all the majesty of God's creation, been so beautiful and the rutted dirt road so smooth. Even as he crossed over the bridge of the bone-dry floodplain and felt the extreme heat, it all seemed glorious. It was so typical of God, who delighted in doing things in ways we would never dream, to have answered this prayer in the wee hours of the morning . . . the *tomorrow* prayed for.

As Dr. Suresh arrived, the entire village was quiet and no one was up and about at this hour. A rooster crowed and a faraway dog barked. He went to the doorway of Vasentha's family *zhopadi* and called, "Vasentha, *nindar may say-ooth,* get up, get up. You need to get ready. *Yeshu* has answered our prayers and you will be able to attend school TODAY."

Groggily, Vasentha came out of the *zhopadi,* but soon the realization of what the doctor had said sunk in. He was going to get to continue attending school.

The doctor explained about the phone call while he helped Vasentha clean up and get ready for school.

"*Chelo, chelo,* hurry up, let's go," Dr. Suresh kept saying to Vasentha.

Finally, they were ready to load the old red promised bicycle on the motorcycle and head for his

51

first day at the new school. What a sight . . . flat tires turning in the wind on each side of the motorcycle as it caused small poofs of dust to rise in the air. The excitement was not hampered by the uncomfortable ride with a bicycle between the man and boy.

Upon arrival at the school, Dr. Suresh was able, after a long discussion, to convince the headmistress that he would return within a couple of hours with enough *rupees* for all the fees. That meant a seventy-kilometer round trip to Prakash for India and back. He then had to navigate the busy hum of Nagpur City to take the bicycle to  the repair shop. He spent all day on his blessed Hero Honda 100 over two hundred kilometers of travel, but it was one of the best days of his life with the joy of seeing God work miracles.

Chapter 13:
Unnecessary Christmas Gift

At Christmas time, Prakash for India gave Dr. Suresh some extra money for his Vet-Med Outreach. There were so many ways he could use the funds and he spent many hours agonizing over what would be the best way to use *God's* money. Finally, he bought a portable PA system. When he emailed Nani, her first reaction was, "What were you thinking? You don't have to amplify your voice to the small groups of people to whom you minister."

Within a few days she was proven to be so totally wrong. Vasentha had gone to the headmistress of his new school and told her about the wonderful Dr. Suresh and felt that he could speak to all three hundred fifty students.

The doctor did this the next month and the newly purchased PA system was extremely helpful.

The next Christmas, Vasentha illustrated his visualization of the manger scene from the Bible story in Luke. To his great surprise, it was used as the Christmas card for Prakash for India that year. Just think—a poor, deprived village boy's colored-pencil drawing being sent all over America.

Chapter 14:
Self-Reliant Training

Things became increasingly desperate for the bird-catcher village. Each day the amount of captured birds grew smaller and smaller, and with the government-enforced wildlife conservation restrictions on hunting any wild animals, it simply meant no food for the entire village. The village men resorted to making a kind of moonshine liquor called *daru*—illegally. This economic venture still did not provide for the basic needs of the four villages and eighteen-thousand-plus members of the *Paradhi* tribe in the Nagpur district. The resulting disaster was extremely heavy on Dr. Suresh's heart. There had to be some way for these dear people to eke out a legal and sustainable living.

After years of planning, Dr. Suresh wrote and started teaching a curriculum called Self-Reliant Training. This was a program of learning the skills of raising goats and chickens and caring for cattle, along with Starting Point[7] biblical principles curriculum designed for young men just like Vasentha who have questions about the Christian faith

If only I could qualify for this program, maybe I could learn to take care of goats and chickens. Of course, you have to have goats and chickens to take care of, thought Vasentha laughingly.

The Self-Reliant curriculum was designed to last six weeks, and Vasentha would be living on the farm with other boys, where the training would take place. He had never spent a night away from his village.

He wondered if this would be something he could handle.

After mustering up all his courage, he shyly approached Dr. Suresh and asked, "Can I become a member of the Self-Reliant class that will be studying during the summer recess?"

Dr. Suresh then made his dream come crashing down when he said, "I don't think I can run the training this summer because there are no funds available."

This was when Vasentha remembered how *Yeshu* had answered the prayers about his going to school, so he began to pray.

Again, miracle of miracles, the funds came from Prakash for India, and Vasentha, along with six other boys from different villages in the area, began his summer of Self-Reliant Training.

This became a life-changing time in Vasentha's young life. He not only truly came to know goatery, but also, because of the Starting Point studies, began to have a personal relationship with *Yeshu*.

The old farmer, who had allowed Dr. Suresh to use his land, was so impressed with the Self-Reliant training program that he did not charge one *rupee* for the use of his land and buildings. So for six weeks, the boys lived, worked, cooked, and ate three meals a day—a first for many of them—and learned the skill of raising goats and chickens.

The six weeks ended all too soon for Vasentha. He could have lived like this forever. It was the first time in his life that he had not gone to sleep hungry, and he had some real friends now.

Because Vasentha was a tribal boy, Dr. Suresh was able to petition the Indian government on his behalf. The government gave Vasentha two goats and several chickens. It was like getting a million dollars for the village. An unimaginable gift.

Sometime later, the farmer who owned the land where the Self-Reliant training had taken place needed to hire some farm ladies . . . men did not do this kind of weeding and backbreaking work. Vasentha asked Dr. Suresh to find out if some of the women from his village could get these jobs. He knew that his villagers were known to be thieves, but he thought with Dr. Suresh's influence, these women could get the jobs. They did, but after only a few weeks, the furious farmer came storming to Dr. Suresh. These women had indeed stolen many pieces of his farm equipment. When Vasentha found out, he made the

women go to the town and acquire the equipment and then return the equipment to the farmer. They also had to apologize, something they had never before done.

Vasentha was fast becoming the leader of his village. Only his age made it impossible for him to be a *Padhan*.

Goats have two kids about every six months. Before long, Vasentha had a herd of goats and a flock of chickens. The village now had milk, eggs, and cheese—things they had never before had enough *rupees* to purchase. Also, there occasionally was mutton in the curry, not just watered-down *dal*—a kind of lentil used as the sole source of protein.

Chapter 15:
Ya Think!

Vasentha's uncle died, so his aunt and her two children came to live in Vasentha's family *zhopadi*. It did have two rooms, but was only twelve paces by eighteen paces overall. These extra people, along with his growing herd of goats, made for very difficult sleeping arrangements.

One day, Dr. Suresh arrived with the supplies to make bricks. He said, "It is very unsanitary for people and goats to be living together." No kidding! So Vasentha gathered the sober village men and started making bricks out of mud, straw, and cow-dung. In about a week, they had a tiny brick *zhopadi* built for the goats to stay at night.

Dr. Suresh continued to work in the village. One day Vasentha came to him and said, "I need to learn how to give the vaccination shots to the goats myself." Consequently, Dr. Suresh showed him the technique and even gave him a small supply of the medication. Within a week, Vasentha returned with a very sad face. Two of his goats had died. He asked what he had done wrong with remorse. Well, he had given the entire supply of medication to the goats, about three times what they should have received.

Sometimes the learning curve is very slow and hard.

After about a year or so, there was a horrible outbreak of dysentery in goats. All the villages around Vasentha's village were losing ten to twenty goats daily to this disease. Vasentha prayed and prayed that *Yeshu* would protect his goats. He didn't lose a single goat, and his family and the villagers that still didn't know *Yeshu* as Lord and Savior began to think this *Yeshu* was a good thing.

The goats that Vasentha raised supported the entire village. He had learned from Dr. Suresh to have a generous heart, so even the neighboring villages received the benefit of Vasentha's Self-Reliant Training.

Chapter 16:
God Will Provide

When asked if he would find a Christian wife outside of his tribe, Vasentha vehemently said *NO*, to the utter shock of Dr. Suresh. Then he went on to explain, "If I marry outside my tribe, they will cast me out of the village. How would I then ever lead them to *Yeshu*? A wedding out of the tribe is very much a difficult thing to forgive and is considered immoral."

In India, community is so strong that the best way to win the people to *Yeshu* is as a group. Such wisdom from such a young man. He saw what *Yeshu* saw, that the unbelievers were valuable. And who better to win them than one of their own.

Vasentha, being the entrepreneur that he is, realized that the broker who arrived each month at his village to buy a couple of his goats for slaughter was making a lot of *rupees*, so he approached Dr. Suresh. "I have this idea of purchasing a motorcycle. I think we can make it a family project."

Shyly, he continued, "This way I can take the goats into the slaughterhouse in Nagpur and make the extra money for myself." Nothing was as interesting to see as Vasentha and his brother with two live

goats hanging over his motorcycle on the highway to Nagpur.

A heart of compassion had grown in Vasentha, and he convinced his family to adopt a young girl whose family had died. Not only did the family not have room, but also adoption outside the immediate family was unknown to this culture. This very act of kindness was breaking through about ten layers of tradition at once.

Chapter 17:
The Move

As the years passed, Vasentha's village became a shining example of what a life of clean living looked like in a tribal culture. The odors, the filth, the disease-infested, ragged children no longer existed. Other *Paradhi* heads would casually drop by unannounced to take a look-see. How was this change happening? For thousands of years, there had been no change, and now suddenly this village had prosperity way beyond the bounds of what would be deemed possible.

One chief in particular decided it had to do with Vasentha. He manipulated and coerced. Vasentha finally moved his entire family to the other *Paradhi* village with the understanding that Vasentha could begin to teach the villagers about living their lives as followers of *Yeshu*. He took it as a challenge to be the first missionary to other villages of his *Paradhi* tribe.

Brick by brick, the old mud-brick *zhopadi* was dismantled and moved to the new village. The Chief had given Vasentha and his family a plot as part of the agreement. Slowly and with care, the new house was built. This time there was careful precision taken and the roof was a luxurious, handmade, sunbaked tile. Vasentha's *maa* sat day after day mixing the red mud and placing it on her thigh to obtain the needed half-round shape and then laying it in the sun to dry. Instead of the cow-dung floor, a new concrete floor was installed— bucketful by bucketful. All the family became involved and excitement grew as the structure began to take shape.

As the moving day approached, the old village head expressed his anger. He now realized that the "*Prakash*" (light) of the village was leaving. Would the children continue to follow the example of Vasentha? To the demise of the village and out of jealous anger, he forbade Dr. Suresh from ever entering the village again.

It took several months before Vasentha thought it was safe for Dr. Suresh to enter his new village. The men were very combative and they had never allowed strangers to enter. Only because of their keen respect for Vasentha did they consent to this doctor's visit. They were very concerned that he would bring the police with him. They knew that their *daru* winemaking business was illegal. Most of the men were drunk all day, every day. The government men knew to stay away from these violent tribal men.

His brow creased with worry, Dr. Suresh told himself that he was a doctor; his compassion was natural. Still with much trepidation, knowing God was his protector, Dr. Suresh made his first visit to the new *Paradhi* village with the same-looking battered mishmash of mud-brick *zhopadi* and shacks. Some roofs were thatched, others tiled, with gaping holes in them. With nerves a-tingle, he was overwhelmingly aware of the hostile looks from the village men as he gingerly navigated the rutted, trash-strewn surface. Two younger men, including a defiant-looking one, crouched in the low entrance to a *zhopadi*.

A lineup of unwashed humanity narrowed the pathway and made the doctor's stiff, plastered smile difficult to maintain. His nostrils were assaulted by the rancid odors of sewer and the ground (cluttered with litter) was wet and uneven under the motorcycle tires.

The doctor was barely off from his motorcycle when Vasentha ran forward with the now-customary hug of welcome for the extraordinary visitor. Again, this tribe had never observed the "hugging thing."

To the doctor's utter surprise, Vasentha had almost finished a very nice tile-roofed brick home. A pile of mud bricks hinting at the hut's future ambitions was blocking the entrance. It was the biggest dwelling in the village with the exception of the Chief's.

Vasentha's *maa* stood in the doorway as Dr. Suresh arrived. She was bathed and her hair was damp from being freshly washed. A shy but clean sister stood just inside the tidy, two-room home, its bright-green walls covered with large posters of Hindu gods, along with one of Christ. Indian culture is never devoid of religious symbols; they are one and the same. Many *Yeshu* followers fear they will no longer be Indian if they become Christian.

"Here is a chair for you, Doctor," said Vasentha. "I went to the city to purchase it just for this visit." The cackle of hens and the bark of a dog were heard in the background. As the doctor sat, a deluge of humanity spilled into the only opening in the shelter, making the room, kept barely cool by a fan whirling overhead, dark and suffocating. The electricity was pilfered from the nearby village with a single wire lying on the ground running through a field.

Suddenly, the scattering of the inquisitive crowd announced the arrival of the Chief. Arms crossed over his chest, long skinny legs planted ungracefully apart, he simply stared at the doctor. Vasentha shyly made the formal introductions, and then offered the Chief a seat on the nearby cot. With a cough, Dr. Suresh finally broke the silence. With the confidence of being a village boy, he began what soon became a lively conversation. The Chief was amazed that this *Marathi* man could speak the tribal language so fluently. Eventually, and with traditional flair, tea was served in the customary small, silver-colored metal cup . . . steaming with a mixture of tea, milk, and, due to the village's poverty, only a smidgen of sugar.

Actually, no business in India is ever conducted until tea is served. Dr. Suresh thought, *Nani would be so upset with me for drinking village tea. She has written me over and over not to take the chance. It is the number-one source of typhoid. But if I offend the Chief on this first important visit, my ministry here will be at an end.*

God, please protect this foolish act, he silently prayed.

With much ado and fanfare, the visit ended after an hour, with an unconditional invitation to return anytime.

Trancelike, Dr. Suresh rode, without notice, down the rutted path atop dirt mounds formed by muck excavated from the winding drainage ditch. Unnoticed were the fields of soft green grain waving in the gentle breeze. Other fields, a multi-designed carpet of the yellow and orange marigold flowers (used to be meticulously sewn together to create the time-honored Indian ceremonial garland) splashed their vibrant colors heavenward. Not until the chaotic convergence of dirt, asphalt, and traffic, and nearly colliding with a bullock cart, did Dr. Suresh snap out of his reverie. God had opened such a door today that it overwhelmed and humbled the good doctor. He could hardly wait to return home and tell Nupi of the day's events. That night, a long, exuberant, detailed email was sent to Nani and Papi in America.

Now the weekly visit became a greatly anticipated occurrence. Gradually, the whole demeanor of the village changed. Filth-encrusted bodies became washed and clean. Hair was being cut and the trash-strewn walkways became tidier.

Chapter 18:
Vacation Bible School

As summer approached, Vasentha remembered the grand times of fun at his former village, so he requested a Vacation Bible School be held for these village children. Due to the fact that strangers were still not welcomed, Dr. Suresh enlisted the help of his wife and daughters. Preparations were made:

a small twig and tarp pergola-like structure was built to somewhat shade the designated area, and a ragged carpet was absconded from a nearby village's *zhopadi* for the children to sit on. Promises were made of daily snacks for the weeklong event.

Dr. Suresh and Nupi prepared the much-used *Veggie Tales* curriculum, years ago donated by Twin Lakes Church in America. The use of these materials had once so transformed a village it had won the coveted award as the cleanest village in all of India. That was the doctor's hope for this upcoming occasion—clean hearts and a clean village.

As the sun rose, bringing the ferocious heat of May, excitement could not be deterred. As the doctor and his family arrived at the village, the children were all awaiting them in restrained jubilance . . . giggling in the common language of kids.

The doctor remembered the initial days when it was very hard to initiate any talk with these people except for Vasentha. Nobody was friendly. *But today they respect me as a man of* Yeshu, Dr. Suresh mused. Vasentha had threatened expulsion from the glorious event if discipline became an issue.

Jaldi, jaldi (hurry, hurry) was the only word to break the silence. As the children wiggled and squirmed, vying for better seats, Dr. Suresh started the program with a song. Tediously, his two girls began the session of teaching the action song to the children. Intertwined with the story were visual aids, things never before dreamed of by these tribal kids. Coloring sheets were handed out and their masterpieces, upon completion, were promptly displayed with honor in each *zhopadi*.

Nupi, with hankie in hand, continued to wipe the trickling sweat from her always-smiling mocha-colored face with those shiny white teeth. *Oh, it is so worth the discomfort to see these grinning faces listening with rapt attention to the stories of* Yeshu's *love,* she ruminated.

More and more children arrived each day as word spread of the astonishing activities taking place in the *Paradhi* village. As the Chief observed the beaming faces, he was reluctant to deny the outsiders. Much to his chagrin, the *daru*-making for the week was almost at a halt, as eight to ten adult men stood each day on the periphery of the event and scrutinized it, looking totally unconcerned but actually listening very carefully to the Bible stories being told.

Daru, made from a small berry growing wild in the nearby jungle, the only source of income for the entire settlement. *Daru* was truly a misnomer, as the concoction was more of a "white lightning" than wine. It was totally and completely illegal; still, with the government restrictions on hunting, it was the only alternative they felt they had . . . another reason for the complete isolation of the village from outsiders, even the police.

Chapter 19:
Forgiveness

Nani and Papi could hardly contain their excitement at the prospect of visiting Vasentha's new village. Not only had they not seen Vasentha in ages, but they also desired to see his sister. She had become pregnant out of wedlock. This meant she was instantly ostracized from the village. She and the young man had become familiar while tending goats in the jungle. The Chief had allowed them to build a thatched shanty *zhopadi* out of twigs and weeds several hundred feet away from the village. The only path leading to the structure was the "toilet alley" for the villagers, which was covered with the *dunga* of every man, woman, and child in the village. Vasentha and his family were not allowed to speak or even go near the young couple, who by now were considered married.

The trek on one of the most deteriorated so-called roads was one of white-knuckled hands clinging to the seat in front, but Nani, Papi, Nupi and Suresh forged onward with the hope of bring about some kind of reconciliation. As Nani stepped out of the car, she grabbed Suresh's arm with her heart skittering and said, "Are you sure this is safe?"

While walking through the rows of barrels where the "wine" was being made, Nani saw many of the small kids in their "God-

clothes," but by the time she left, they were dressed in their finest.

The hostility in the eyes of the drunken young men standing with arms crossed and belligerent expressions did not exude assurance. They peered at her through bloodshot eyes that were yellowed by the ever-present liver disintegration. Although they were slight, they gave the impression of wiry strength.

A man with orange-red hair dyed with henna stood staring. It was quite obvious he had never before seen a white-skinned, blonde-haired woman.

Pongs, filth, and sickness infested this village. Ragged children came running, pointing and giggling. Flies covered the sores of the lame. Smoke from dung-fueled fires filled the air. Stepping carefully over excrement, stones, and whatever else covered the path made the short walk seem like miles—*not a trip for the cowardly.* Then, with a burst of joy, Vasentha walked up and hugged Papi. Two young girls, grinning from ear to ear, presented skimpy traditional yellow-and-gold marigold floral garlands. Bending their heads down, Nani and Papi received the tribute to a thunder of clapping. Their fear-riddled bodies began to relax. Still, when one very drunk young man, his breath smelling of raw alcohol, tried to grab Nani, it made for an unpleasant altercation.

A tea ceremony is always necessary before any dealings can be accomplished. And knowing the village tea would not be acceptable to the Western stomach, Nupi had thoughtfully prepared a delicious, very sweet, milky tea mixture for all to enjoy, even providing small use-and-toss plastic cups.

Even though the *zhopadi* was changed radically in cleanliness, Nani still opted for the plastic chair instead of the cloth-covered bed. The plastic chair was quickly dusted with a dirty rag. Papi took the bed. This village had electricity, but the whirling fan did little to alleviate the stifling heat. Gradually, the room darkened as more and more faces appeared in the diminutive doorway opening, cutting off all outside air from entering the small structure's room. A myriad of big, chocolate-drop eyes stared at the unusual foreigners.

Slowly, the villagers began to answer the questions and asked some of their own. "Where do you come from? How did you get here?" Having never seen a white person, they also found the skin and Nani's hair color a great marvel. The Chief said he had seven daughters.

Nani asked, "Could one of the girls become chief when you die?" It was then she felt the tripwires that surrounded them in the Indian tribal culture. *Absolutely NO!* He would simply get a new wife and continue to try for a boy. He didn't realize he shot the gender bullets.

Paramount on the agenda—after the ceremonial tea, of course—was visiting the young ostracized couple that had been thrown out of the tribe. Nobody sat with them; nobody touched them; nobody ate food made by them. They had to go outside the community and live their lives without any relationship or support from the village. In a communal society, this was the worst kind of punishment.

First and foremost was receiving the Chief's permission. Dr. Suresh had such a phenomenal way with these people, so permission was freely given. Their trust in him was evident.

After exiting the small hut, Nani and Nupi began carefully picking their way along the path strewn with "golden fertilizer." Before Nani knew what was happening, the girl's mother was alongside, crying. Knowing the mother would not understand her, Nani asked, "Nupi, what is the problem?"

"She has never been allowed to come this far on the path or even look upon her daughter. The Chief, because of you, is allowing her to come. She cannot touch, but can at least see."

With instant sympathy, Nani embraced the tiny, weather-beaten woman. They continued to walk with Nani's arm around the slumped shoulders of a body thin from lack of enough food.

The crowd of onlookers and visitors approached the wee, pitiful hut of thatched fabrication, poles interwoven with willowy branches, withed twigs, and grass reeds. Other slender poles lay on the roof to support the thatch and forlorn scraps of discarded rubbish. There stood the shy couple with the two goats Dr. Suresh had been allowed to gift them at Christmas. Without the goats the young couple would have most likely perished.

Nani immediately went forward, enfolded the young woman in a hug, and patted her now-extended belly—not at all the custom of the villagers. Many photos were taken and Papi and the Chief engaged in deep conversation as Dr. Suresh interpreted. The ghastly conditions were even worse when it was found that the couple was not staying in the shack because a poisonous snake had invaded during the previous week. Wiping away her tears, Nani stooped down and entered the small hut. The geckos scuttled in the thatch. Dust images danced and swirled as the sun filtered through the sparsely woven twigs, allowing all other elements to intrude on the small space.

How can they survive in these conditions? she thought. "Show me your home," she said to the young mother-to-be. She encouraged the young bride to enter in order to overcome her fear and then maybe resume using the *zhopadi* for shelter. The entire wealth of the couple was wrapped in two blankets discreetly tucked in the corner. The small reed divider wall that gave a semblance of a two-room home fascinated Nani. She let the undernourished girl show her with pride how the intricately woven wall was constructed.

Meanwhile, Papi was asking the Chief, "What will it take to restore this young couple to the village? They will die without help."

The Chief explained, "They committed immoral thing. If at all they want us to forgive them, they must go through the only process possible in three phases.

"First, the family that is punished sacrifices a goat. They can purchase it from market. Then they prepare mutton curry without any vegetables and *chapattis*, enough to feed the whole village and heads of other ten nearby villages. Also, the young couple cannot touch any of the sacrificial animals. Then we will allow the punished people to come and stay in the village, but still treat them as untouchables.

"Two—a penalty must be paid of minimum twenty thousand *rupees* to start the sacrificial ceremony. My father, who all heads and villagers consider as their priest or judge, can decide place for sacrifice and worship to the south. We think god lives in the south direction. We begin by cleaning the goat with water and cow-dung, then give holy bath to goat. The judge with his special knife will slit the throat of the goat and then other people in the committee help in slaughtering the animal, offering the head of the animal to god. Then there is a ceremony where the blood is drawn and spread on the fire."

He held up three fingers to emphasize the points.

"Three—again, they have to collect money and buy an unblemished full-grown male buffalo, roast the animal on a spit, all the villagers and heads from all ten villages eat the meat . . . approximately seven hundred people. After this ceremony, they can be totally forgiven."

Astounded by how much the processes and requirements for redemption were like Old Testament blood and animal sacrifices, Papi, in shock, said, "That is impossible! Is there not some way to forgive and help restore the young couple without such a huge, unobtainable cost?"

The Chief was intently interested in the process that the white *Saheb* would recommend.

"What you have told me is an impossible task for this young couple to accomplish in their entire lifetime," said the *Saheb* with concern. "If the whole village were to be involved in helping to make the required restitution happen, it would be more significant and important for everyone. Then forgiveness could also happen in a timely fashion. Every person would feel they had a part in the momentous occasion. Our *Yeshu* would want the young couple to repent also, but he would want a heart change, not sacrifices."

"Your way is very much better. I will try to find a way that we can restore them without offending the other elders and heads," replied the Chief.

Within the months before the birth of the little boy child, restoration was accomplished—to everyone's satisfaction.

Chapter 20:
Picnic Visit

The following year, in the month of August, on another harrowing trek down the rutted pathway, a small entourage from Prakash for India visited the isolated village. Anticipating a long day, they had packed a picnic lunch. The sky was a perfect pale blue, while billowy clouds leisurely floated unhindered. Seeing a landscape that was normally so brown and desolate transformed into a clean, lush, green countryside with overflowing streams and ponds was overwhelming to Nani and Papi.

They were shocked to see a freshly paved narrow road, but were reminded of the recent political election and that the politicians had, in order to get votes, instigated this new luxury.

The day was sunny and warm, so before entering the village, it was decided they would stop and eat the picnic lunch the Prakash cook, Sunil, had so lovingly provided.

Finding a spot where they could eat undisturbed was the trick. Just around the bend in the road from a farm was a concrete ford over the rivulet. Picture perfect! Lush green vegetation provided much-needed shade. Sunlight sifted through the branches of the overhanging trees, gliding the water pooled in low spots of the riverbed. Laying out old newspaper sheets on the small concrete ford, they arranged the lunch.

There were carefully made cheese sandwiches, fried chicken, bananas, and biscuits . . . indication of British English terminology. Only a few humongous black ants invaded the idyllic meal. All around the birds were singing and the gargantuan, leathery, heart-shaped leaves of the tropical *arum* plants swayed in a gentle breeze . . . a welcomed relief from the hustle and bustle of the city.

Deciding a barefoot walk in the stream would greatly reduce the heat, Nani plunged in, which began a riot of splashing as everyone else rushed in. Then the group collected quartz crystals from the lava flow along the side of the minuscule stream.

Excitingly, just then, the forest jungle manager came by on his brand-new motorcycle and disturbed the frolicking group. But Papi was beyond thrilled when he found out the man was tracking a tiger he had spotted close by the day before. Seeing a tiger in the wild was one of Papi's lifelong dreams.

After loading all the remnants of the lunch into the *Qualis* and continuing toward the village, Dr. Suresh realized the young man he could see wrapped in his white muslin *dhoti,* tilling the nearby field with a wooden plough and two large white bullocks, their hides glistening in the noonday sun, was a former student of Vet-Med's Self-Reliant program.

The car was ordered to stop and the men jumped out to navigate the ploughed field. Nani's brain could not compute what her eyes were seeing. The young man was using an ancient form of cultivating his field while talking on his cell phone. *It's astonishing,* she thought. *I can't believe it. This is India,* she reminded herself, *the land of contrast.*

Papi would have loved to get behind those bullocks, just to try it, but the driver, Premdas, beat him to the punch. It was fun when you didn't have to do it every day.

While the women waited for the men to return to the car, Rachael teasingly used one of the teak tree's gargantuan leaves as a fan for Nani.

Later, as the entourage continued down the narrow paved road, the trees became taller and denser, closing out all view of the sky. Tiny green parrots flitted back and forth across the road. Nani's artist's heart wanted to stop and sketch every picturesque scene.

Continuing to drive to the village, the group realized just how far the young farmer must travel every day with the bullocks just to get to the fields. He and his father worked seven days a week for at least eight hours just to bring in a good crop of soybeans. The young farmer then had to tend his goats when he returned to his *zhopadi*.

As many times as Nani had seen the incomprehensible contrasts in India, she felt the next surprise took the cake. As the group entered the village, there sat a satellite dish on top of one of the *zhopadi*! The villagers might not have enough food, but they had a dish! Things like this became huge status symbols, even if the apparatus did not operate.

Upon their arrival this time, the village buzzed with excitement. The onerous young men were attentive but not combative. After participating in the necessary ceremonial teatime, Nani was asked to name the newly restored young couple's baby boy. Ranni had waited to name her child, wanting the honor of letting Nani do it. Total forgiveness for the young couple was easier with the birth of a boy. If the child had been a girl, the restoration would have been harder.

"Well, let me think," said Nani, as she cuddled the naked bottom in her hands, "I think I'll name him Connor after my grandson in America." Little did she know that her grandson would be in heaven in just a few short years. The village was thrilled with the American name, letting the new sound roll off tongues unaccustomed to this language. Their chattering and raucous laughter made Nani wish she understood their tribal language.

What will this world be like for future generations? she wondered. All they had known was a life of drudgery and hunger. The power to choose one's fate was only the prerogative of the wealthy.

As the entourage was ready to leave, the Chief approached Papi and said, "Do you know about this kind of fake light that is very good, you see far, far away? I have heard there is machine with a bright light. If we had such light, we could hunt the wild animals at night without so much trouble."

Trying to decipher the meaning of the Chief's words, finally Papi understood. Turning to Dr. Suresh, he said, "O . . . kay, I get it. Does he mean a flashlight, or torch as you call it?"

An ensuing conversation between the doctor and the Chief revealed that indeed he wanted a torch.

"Well, I just happen to have a five-battery black Mag-Lite flashlight in my room back on the Prakash campus. Let's set up a date to return at night and I will give him the torch and show him how to use it," instructed Papi.

A night the following week was decided upon.

Chapter 21:
The Torth

Never having ventured into the jungle at night, they found the arduous trip over the bumpy, rutted, potholed road traumatic. Not a jaunt for the coward. The night sky was aglow with a myriad of stars clearly seen because of the lack of ambient light surrounding such a vast area. Finally, in the far distance, a total of three tiny lights were seen . . . one being a strand of flashing, colored *Diwali* lights. A single light bulb shining in all its glory announced the final destination. Gingerly the vehicle slowed to a halt where the road was too narrow to drive any further. Surveying the black surroundings, the group of five carefully descended from the car.

The single bulb spreading its wan globes of light showed Vasentha and the Chief waiting expectantly for the car to arrive. The Chief met the car and grabbed Papi's arm, leaving Nani to fend for herself. With her heart pounding furiously, Nani lowered herself from the car, at the risk of life and limb. The realization of what was on the path and what she might step into stunned her. *Be still my fluttering heart,* she commanded her thoughts.

"Sur-resh," she warned as she aggressively attached herself to his arm, "you know if I step in any 'golden fertilizer' or cow-dung, I will be very upset." Knowing from experience what an unpleasant experience it would be.

Laughing, Suresh slowly negotiated the unevenly trodden track and they arrived in front of Vasentha's hut unscathed. Hordes of dirty children and adults surrounded the visitors. The demonstration "ceremony" of the coveted torch began and the Chief could hardly contain his excitement. A smile from brown ear to brown ear illuminated his face while white teeth glistened even in the dim light. "No one has ever loved us like you do," he uttered. The reality of everyday life in India without running water, ample electricity, or toilet facilities made this gift all the more precious. Of course, Papi would probably be expected to supply batteries for many years to come.

Wanting to show off his new treasure, the Chief (with Vasentha behind) jumped on his motorcycle and motioned for the foreigners to follow. Nani thought, *Well, silly me; I thought we were ready to go back to the car and Prakash, not yet another village? Where on earth are we going now?* But, with a lot of jabber, she found out they were off to the Chief's brother-in-law's village.

Papi said, "He needs to show his new torch to his wife. They just had another baby girl. That makes nine." As was the custom on the last day of *Diwali*, brothers and sisters stayed together.

"He keeps trying to have a boy and has no comprehension of the fact that he is the reason for all the girls," replies Suresh laughingly.

So off into the black night on winding roads, following the faint headlight, they pursued the Chief. The Chief, with his "torch" flashing, continued to direct the way. It was hard to enjoy the beauty of the evening star and the pale shape of the crescent moon. They hit pothole after pothole in the road; then, as they rounded a bend, they almost ran into a bullock. The vehicle lurched sideways and Nani's knuckles were again white as she clutched the back of the driver's seat. "Wooeee, that was close!" she exclaimed.

They drove down a road that had been decaying for a decade and was waiting forlornly for construction. This pathway truly was never intended for a car. On one side a woman squatted in front of her tiny, crumbling cow-dung home, shelling peas.

On the other side, a long piece of wood poked out of a fire, making the passage of the car impossible.

At last the Chief stopped and jumped off his motorcycle, indicating this was the settlement. The  village, like most, was lacking in electricity, and the one doorway where light was spilling forth was encased in a mass of flaming bougainvillea, giving the small dwelling the distinction of wealth.

For the second time, the Chief grabbed Papi's hand and again Nani grabbed Suresh. This time they at least had a little light, but the ground was muddy and sticky underfoot. Upon arrival at the mud house, a man quickly came out of the crowd of people and gave Papi a bear-hug. Then, to her absolute amazement, he gave Nani one, too, leaving red "*holy kumkum*" powder all over her cheek. *NEVER in all the years I have been in India has a strange man given me a hug,* she mused. An Indian man hugging a foreigner had never happened before. *Well, I guess they have heard about this "hugging thing" from Vasentha,* reasoned Nani. The man was the brother of the Chief's wife.

The group was ushered into the house with ceremonial flair. The displaying and demonstration of the torch, along with lively conversation, went on and on until finally Nani asked, "Where is the baby?" A woman, most likely the mother, in traditional Indian dress (a knee-length tunic with side slits worn over loose trousers and an embroidered scarf draped across her shoulders) jumped up and went over to the corner behind a cot. She lifted a tiny infant from the floor—all five pounds of her. Unable to keep her hands off of the baby, Nani demonstrated that she wanted to hold the diminutive, adorable child. Placing the newborn on her lap, she let her finger be clasped by the dark-skinned miniature ones. The small female child fit perfectly on her lap with her hands cradling the wee head and bare bottom. Cooing and stretching, the infant began to excrete a warm liquid. *Oh my, what do we have here? How can such a teeny-tiny wee one have so much pee?* questioned Nani without verbalizing. *OH MY GOSH! I have just been initiated.*

Papi laughed, "Well, at least it was filtered water."

The family was mortified and wanted to take the baby immediately away.

Nani implored, "No, no, her bladder is empty, so no more damage . . . well, hopefully, no more."

Suresh laughingly said, "She has welcomed you wholeheartedly."

Nani thought, *God, can I get some help here? How can I extricate myself from the problem without causing any further embarrassment?* Thankfully, no one seemed to notice the dark discoloration of Nani's jeans as the group rose to leave, but the laughing was without cease on the drive back to Prakash. *Oh well, jeans will wash—beating them on a rock in the distinctive Indian custom,* mused Nani.

Chapter 22:
The Schedule

As Dr. Suresh was exiting his home, he had an overwhelming feeling that he needed to go to Vasentha's village. Why was *Yeshu* telling him to go? His day was completely scheduled. He had many important things to attend to. As he was riding his motorcycle out of the enclave, the feeling would not go away. So, begrudgingly, he turned and headed for the outlying village.

"You know, Lord, this is messing up my schedule for the whole week!"

The roads seemed to be more congested than ever. The doctor's countenance showed every bit of his aggravation at the disruption to his carefully planned schedule.

Upon his arrival at the primitive mud *zhopadi* village (which had no cell phones, minimal access to TV, and no awareness about health), there was an abnormal stillness. The doctor's senses were on high alert.

Quickly, he walked to Vasentha's mud-brick *zhopadi*. As he entered, he saw the local medicine man chanting and sprinkling water with a wet broom over Vasentha's limp body.

Oh, Yeshu, *forgive me*, thought the doctor.

Now he could see why *Yeshu* had guided him to the village.

What if he had not listened?

The consequences were beyond imagination. One look at Vasentha told the doctor that the young man was near death. The small room reeked of body odor. Vasentha had not taken a bath for several days, nor had he eaten or had a proper amount of clean water.

The doctor began to ask questions and, finally, with much coaxing, the story was revealed.

Vasentha had gone on his usual daily trip to get firewood from the jungle nearby. Heavily perspiring, he returned home—the scorching sun overhead— with a heavy load of wood on his head. As he came into the *zhopadi*, he felt a little weak, but it seemed normal. However, during the night, he developed a high fever. The village people think fever in the summer season is mostly because of heat stroke.

Vasentha's *maa* had also been using the wet-broom technique on him with all the incantations and expected him to get better by the next day. But that didn't happen. The fever continued, and along with it came severe body aches, chills, and nausea. Vasentha remained in bed, eating very little. His condition became worse each day. He had severe headaches and fever, and every joint in his body swelled and ached to the point that he was unable to move. Vasentha had a serious infection and it needed immediate attention.

After helping Vasentha off his floor bed, Dr. Suresh, with the help of two young men, tried to sit Vasentha on the motorcycle, but he was too weak to hold on. So, forgetting all traffic rules (only two people on a motorcycle), the doctor procured one of the young men to sit with him on the motorcycle, holding Vasentha in the middle. They travelled eighteen kilometers in the sweltering heat to reach the government hospital in *Kalmeshwar*.

Of course, they could not see the doctor right away, as the hospital was jam-packed with people with similar symptoms. When the government doctor finally examined Vasentha after several hours of waiting, he asked, "Have you been bitten by a mosquito?"

"Mosquito bite?" Vasentha said, laughing. "What is unusual about that? We live among the mosquitoes. We are immune to them!"

The doctor then took blood samples to test and another session of waiting began. Finally the tests confirmed that it was *chikungunya*.

Chikungunya (chik-un-GUN-yuh) is a virus transmitted by mosquitoes that causes the sudden onset of fever and severe joint pain. Other signs and symptoms may include fatigue, muscle pain, headache, and rash. Signs and symptoms of chikungunya usually appear two to seven days after being bitten by an infected mosquito.

No vaccine exists to prevent the chikungunya virus, and there's no effective antiviral treatment. The disease runs a limited course and can be fatal. Treatment is aimed at relieving symptoms with rest, fluids, and medications.[8]

The doctor prescribed some medicines to be taken for two weeks and gave an admonition about how close to death the young man truly was.

Without concern for his personal budget, the good doctor Suresh bought the medicines and took Vasentha back home. He waited to make sure the fatigued patient was comfortable on the floor bed, wanting to give Vasentha his first dose of medicine in his presence. He was doubtful that Vasentha would take the medicine properly. The drug could not be taken on an empty stomach, so orders were given for food to be prepared.

Eventually, the cooked food arrived. It was rice and some watery curry, looking completely red from the use of a huge amount of chili. Smiling, Vasentha's *maa* brought the plate in front of Vasentha, and he stared miserably at the plate and forlornly at the doctor.

He said, "My throat and stomach-ache are too much to eat this. Give me only the medicine. I will swallow it."

The doctor asked, "Is there any milk in the house?"

"No!" was the answer, with a look of "How could he even think that was a possibility?"

"Okay. Then cook some *sooji* (a rice mush), so he can swallow the medicine," commanded the doctor.

Maa stood there as if she had heard nothing.

Now the doctor was getting a little impatient. He wanted to give Vasentha the medicine soon. His entire schedule was totally interrupted.

With aggravation showing in his voice, Dr. Suresh asked, "What's the matter? Make some *sooji*!"

"We don't have any *sooji* in the house" was the answer. "Nor is there any milk or sugar."

Again the reality of the destitution of these dear people hit the doctor square in the face. He begged their forgiveness and then took his motorcycle and travelled quite some distance to get *sooji*, sugar, and some milk—enough to last for a few days until Vasentha got better.

After the doctor returned, Vasentha's *maa* made the *sooji*. He ate it with gusto and then took his medicine.

Before leaving, Dr. Suresh gave detailed instructions to Vasentha's *maa*. "Give him this same medicine every four hours, exactly like I did," he told her, and then promised to return the next day.

By then, the sky was a brilliant red hue with the setting of the summer sun, God's paintbrush in action. Again the gravity of the day leapt to the forefront of the doctor's thoughts.

What a great cost there would have been for disobedience! Vasentha could have died had I waited till my scheduled visit.

Daily visits to the village were made in the beginning, and on alternate days when Vasentha started recovering.

After a week, as the doctor arrived, he saw Vasentha on his floor bed reading his Bible. The young man said, "This sickness has given me more time to read the Bible. I think I need to be baptized. I need to show everyone I am a follower of *Yeshu*."

Dr. Suresh stood before the young man in awe— and to think his schedule might have interfered with *Yeshu's* schedule!

Vasentha recovered and was back to his regular occupation of goat herding.

Chapter 23:
Miracle Girl for Vasentha

Vasentha's herd of goats began to grow, as did his esteem in the village. The age for matrimony was fast approaching and pressure was coming from all sides. His resolve to marry only a Christian girl, and one of his tribe, seemed to be an impossible task. Due to the fact that his father was a drunk, Vasentha's uncle and the Chief continued to bring opportunities to his attention that he would deny after only two questions. "Is she quarrelsome and is she a Christian?"

"How do you know she is a quarrelsome girl?" Nani asked. Matter-of-factly, Vasentha stated, "By looking in her eyes." Nani thought she knew what he meant. Indians are unable to hide in their eyes their honest feelings.

As the word got out through the *Paradhi* communities, finally a girl was found . . . miracle of miracles . . . a fourth in the life of young Vasentha.

Sheshi lived in a village that was about two hundred kilometers away from Vasentha's village but was still a part of the *Paradhi* tribe. Her acceptance of *Yeshu* as her Savior had come years before, when as a small girl she had attended a Vacation Bible School held in a nearby village. Her acceptance was genuine, but there had been no growth because there were no Christian materials in her language. No one ever followed up to disciple the young girl. The evangelist never returned. She had so enjoyed the stories of *Yeshu* and the coloring pages that still hung with honor on the walls of her parents' *zhopadi*. Because Vasentha had broken the educational barrier Sheshi had also attended school.

The introduction ceremony was to take place within a few weeks. Sheshi could hardly contain her excitement. As the day approached, she was warned she must not make eye contact with the young man while she served him tea. It was unusual that permission had been given for her to even be able to serve the tea.

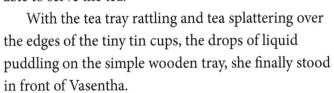

With the tea tray rattling and tea splattering over the edges of the tiny tin cups, the drops of liquid puddling on the simple wooden tray, she finally stood in front of Vasentha.

How could one small glance hurt? she thought. So up came her eyes to view a handsome, thin, light-brown-faced boy. He was not black, which was such a pleasing thing. His fine-looking face made her acceptance much easier . . . not that her opinion would have really counted, but her father had said he would be generous and let her voice her thoughts. Now she served him a cup of tea with a little look, and he accepted the tea with a look of his own.

Vasentha asked her father questions about Christianity and felt good about the responses. It was very uncommon that he would be allowed to have this kind of contact with Sheshi before their engagement, but Vasentha insisted. He said, "I like her." She said in a barely audible voice, "I like him too." That was it—a done deal!

The shy women in the room nudged one another and whispered behind their hands the approval of the pair. The men needed to make a contract and the negotiations of the dowry and marriage arrangements.

As per custom, group approval was necessary. Not just the family. The *Paradhi* tribe looks very simple and poor, but they have very strong and hard traditions—with strict social rules followed by their ancestors. If anybody marries, even in the tribe, without the tribe's and parents' approval, they have to face a long process of reconciliation to come under the tribe once again. So endorsement by the tribe was of utmost importance. Without it they would be banished.

Chapter 24:
Vasentha's Engagement

The tribal engagement was a very long process. If the two families knew each other well, the conversation for "marriage fixing" could be done more quickly. Most of the time, it happened between families having long relations. The parents would start exchanging views about marriage when they would meet other parents . . . like at weddings or in the markets. Vasentha did not have this advantage. His Christian stance was a first for the tribe.

In the earlier days, the opinions of the girl and the boy didn't have any importance, but nowadays parents would take into account their opinions and willingness in deciding the date of the engagement.

There was a ceremonial tea and discussion where the two young people would see each other, and the date of the engagement (called *Shal-mundi*) was decided upon. For this, the parents of both the boy and the girl, along with the village head committee, would come together and decide the appropriate date for *Shal-mundi* based on strict rules and the gods.

On the chosen *Shal-mundi* date, a program was held at the girl's home. Vasentha's family members, along with the heads of both villages, gathered together. The girl's parents had arranged a non-vegetarian lunch for everyone.

Then after worshipping and praising their gods, the *Shal-mundi* program started. In this program, the boy's side had to bring a new *sari* and various other clothing items for the girl. Vasentha then put *sin door*, a red-colored powder, on Sheshi's forehead and gave her the gifts he had brought. Vasentha took great care in choosing the very best gifts he could afford for his future mate. Even though Vasentha and Sheshi were Christians, they were compelled to follow the age-old rituals of the *Paradhi* tribe or risk banishment.

The entire process was repeated the next day at Vasentha's village. The girl's parents brought gift clothes, a watch, and many other items, plus a gold chain for Vasentha. After all the ceremonies were finished, the date of marriage was decided.

In all strata of Indian culture, the "group" makes the decisions. It is always a long process.

Chapter 25:
Midnight Call

Wat on earth? Who could possibly be at our door? thought Dr. Suresh. As he opened the door, he found Vasentha and his mother standing in the early morning light with an invitation for Vasentha's wedding.

"*Aau in, aau in,*" said the kind doctor as he opened the door wide for their entrance.

Shyly, Vasentha said, "I want to call America to invite Papi Sir to my wedding."

It was midnight when the phone rang. "Who could possibly be phoning at this time of night?" Noting the international number, Papi said, "I sure hope there is not an emergency."

"Hello."

"What did you say?"

With all the courage he could muster, Vasentha again said slowly, "Sir, will you come to my wedding?"

Who the caller was was a total mystery. Quickly, Dr. Suresh came on the line and said, "That was Vasentha."

"Vasentha? He doesn't speak English."

For weeks, Vasentha had made a daily trek into Nagpur City. The college student he had coerced into teaching him the English phrase was delighted with his success.

"What? Vasentha, you are speaking English. Of course I will try. When is the wedding?"

At this point Vasentha again relinquished the phone to Dr. Suresh. Questions and answers flew across the international lines. Joy was abundant as the story unfolded of finding a Christian girl for Vasentha to marry. The wedding was to take place on May 20.

"You know, Suresh, Nani made me promise years ago never to return to India in May. I nearly came home in a pine box the last time I was there in May. It is so dreadfully hot, up to a hundred and thirty degrees."

"I know, Papi, but this is Vasentha's request. He has such a big dream of you coming for his marriage."

"Well, the Lord will simply have to provide the funds and give me strength. We will pray. I want to make sure that my attendance will not offend the Chief."

Dr. Suresh assured him the entire tribe was looking forward to his presence.

After such a long phone call, Papi became uneasy about the cost for Nupi and Suresh, so Papi told Nupi, "Let me know how much this call was and I will send some *rupees* to cover the bill."

Nupi said, "Oh, that's OK, we are using Nani's phone." Nani and Papi burst out laughing. God knew Nani needed to leave her phone in India for this very reason.

The next morning, in a flurry of activity, Papi called his American board for approval, which was given with reserved enthusiasm due to the heat. Delta Airlines was contacted for tickets. The short notice made for difficult scheduling. At every snag, a solution was quickly provided, and by the end of the day, all arrangements were in order.

It was hard to believe that the boy, who was just about eight years old when Nani and Papi first met him, was now about to get married.

Chapter 26:
Vasentha's Marriage

The inconceivable had happened; Papi had decided to go to Vasentha's wedding in the hottest month of the year. He arrived on the 19th of May.

On the 20th, the entourage from Prakash for India started at 10:00 a.m. to go to the wedding. Everyone was happy that Papi had arrived . . . not only for his presence, but also because of his air-conditioned car. There'd been one throat-closing, stomach-grinding moment when a lorry going the wrong way on the highway swerved to miss a cow and nearly collided with the *Qualis*.

It was such a long trip and the weather was unbearably hot. Prayers were offered often for Papi and the heat.

. . . .

Vasentha woke very early and called Dr. Suresh for the fifteenth time. "Is he here? Is he coming to my wedding?" he anxiously asked.

Since morning, Suresh's mobile phone had rung almost every fifteen minutes, and it was always Vasentha, giving every detail of his movements and asking if they were going to be there for sure or not.

"Yes, no need for you to worry," Dr. Suresh patiently answered—again.

As the sun began to heat the day, Vasentha looked at his wedding suit. He had never had a complete suit of clothing before in his entire young life. He was not sure where to start. The white suit fabric was easily soiled, and the red shirt was stiff and uncomfortable. Still, with persistence and a deep desire to please, he continued to put on each piece of the appointed clothing.

The brightly colored gold-and-red turban was definitely going to bring streams of sweat running down his face. Grimly, he placed it on his head. As he looked at the shoes, his feet curled with resentment at the thought of such confinement. And because Vasentha unknowingly put them on the wrong feet, they rubbed and caused even more discomfort to the appendages unaccustomed to any footwear except thin rubber *chupples*.

A *Paradhi* marriage ceremony is organized like *Hindu* marriage ceremonies. The boy's family, along with his relatives and their entire village, go to the girl's village. This shows richness by taking or having a great number of vehicles. Vasentha was Christian, but he would not offend the many villagers by not having the traditional *Paradhi* ceremony.

Finally, Papi and his entourage arrived at the village where the wedding was to be held and were welcomed by *berates* waiting at the outskirts of the village. They danced around the car as they played their horns and instruments, their colorful turbans bouncing . . . Vasentha, in his new suit (maybe the first time from head to toe), came and greeted Papi, as did his mother. She, in fact, touched Papi's feet in a sign of blessing and honor. She couldn't say it with words but did say with her actions how thankful she was that he had actually come to the wedding. They could not believe the difference they saw in Vasentha's mother . . . her manners, her way of talking, and her cleanliness. When they'd first started going to his house, Vasentha's mother was so shy she would hardly talk. But now they saw a mature woman who had a lot of insights about life and who had supported her son to change for the better. Vasentha had received a lot of support from his mother.

Then came the rail-thin father . . . completely dressed . . . proud enough to show that he had stayed away from liquor that day. Even though he was slight, he gave the impression of the wiry strength of a jungle dweller. Liquor to him was like oxygen. Papi had never known him to be without liquor and smoking. On this day, everybody normally drinks wine as much as they want. But it was amazing to see and know that Vasentha had informed his village people and the attendees of the marriage that he did not want anyone to drink at his wedding. Strangely, they honored his request. Dr. Suresh sniffed all around the people to see if this was a fact, and really none were found to be drunk.

All occasions are graded for success by the amount and quality of the food served. The girl's parents had to feed about two thousand people. It simply would be unacceptable to eliminate anyone in attendance, whether an invited guest or not.

One by one, the group from Prakash followed Vasentha over a rutted, rock-strewn path to a temple where they could find some shade. Now they needed to just sit and wait until the wedding started. They were on time, but in India time is never a factor, and things will start when they start.

Thankfully, the group had brought snacks, and so they spread out a blanket under the shade of a lonely banyan tree near the temple and enjoyed some refreshment. Premdas, the driver, pulled out a rag of sorts and wrapped it around his head in typical Indian fashion. They believed this would cool the body in the sweltering heat.

As the group was eating and bantering amongst themselves, Vasentha's sister came and invited them to follow her to see the bride's house. The bride was getting ready at the school hall; one of her friends was helping her with her make-up. Her simple, lime-green *sari* with a red *cholie* would be changed for an elaborate red silk *sari* with a gold thread trim, considered extraordinary for a tribal girl.

She wore jewelry in her ears and nose, and around her neck and arms. Pondering her life with Vasentha as layer upon layer of *mehendi* henna was applied in an intricate pattern to her hands and arms, Sheshi was glad *Yeshu* had given her a Christian man for a husband. Somewhere hidden in the intricate design would be her name and Vasentha's. She would look for it during the wedding ceremony.

The group returned to their picnic spot. Runners came to the group's little picnic site and said, "We will start the wedding as soon as the food is ready," only to return thirty minutes later to say, "We will start when the band, the drums, and the trumpets arrive."

Finally, the group was ushered into the multicolored *pendahl*. Sunlight streamed through the cracks in the fabric, highlighting dust-mote-filled air. It was time, and the procession started with music and dancing. Vasentha slowly stepped into a decorated white car—the traditional white horse was not affordable. He felt the luxury of the soft leather seats . . . hot to the touch. *This is my wedding day,* he thought. Slowly, the car drove to the *pendahl* just a few hundred yards away. The rituals at the entrance of the brightly patterned and multi-colored tent seemed to be never-ending, but, ultimately, he entered.

Vasentha strained so hard to see Papi that his eyes hurt. He looked left and right, searching among the throngs of people. He finally saw Papi standing with a huge smile on his face, camera in hand. Now he could relax.

Vasentha took his position on the small red-carpeted platform. Papi quickly took pictures and strained to hold his composure as he saw the brand-new shoes on the wrong feet. *How would Vasentha*

know? he thought. *He has never worn a pair of shoes.*

Already the trickles of sweat were running down Vasentha's back. *Breathe*, he told himself.

The noise of the crowd and the running of children to and fro were not in the least bit distracting. It would not be an Indian wedding without all the chaos. As Vasentha saw Sheshi entering under the red canopy, a smile encased his face. As soon as the bride entered the platform, the pair was told to stand in front of each other and hold up a white gold-trimmed scarf high between them. They were not supposed to see each other.

Again, he told himself, *Breathe.* Yeshu *has given me a beautiful helpmate,* he reasoned.

As soon as the wedding was about to start, the electricity went off. Not to worry; they simply started the tape recorder on a car battery. In the *Paradhi* tribe, most of the time the marriage ceremonies take place with a prerecorded prayer. Traditionally, they do not have a priest available in the jungle because a tribe cannot afford to have an actual priest attend; they simply obtain a prerecorded ceremony. At least they were uncharacteristically prepared for the eventuality of a power outage.

The loud chanting went on and on. Papi stood taking pictures in the front. The colored rice, *akshida,* was thrown all over him. Ten to twelve people gathered around Vasentha on the platform, each telling him and the bride what to do next. The nervous couple followed everything told to them with neat obedience. Everyone was an advisor as to how things should proceed. No one had complete authority. There was no structure or person in charge.

The scarf was lowered and Vasentha placed a heavy orange-and-white floral garland over Sheshi's head. Then Sheshi did the same to Vasentha. She knew traditionally she was supposed to frown and look very sad-faced, but she was too blissful for such an expression. While the garlands were exchanged, the chanting continued. Children played near the platform without any adult being annoyed. At last the young couple sat in the traditional red chairs. At every wedding in India, whether Hindu, Christian, rich, or poor, there will always be decorative red chairs.

Papi, as chief guest, was asked to come to the platform. He prayed a prayer for *Yeshu* to bless the young couple. Vasentha then gifted the time-honored garland of gold and white marigolds over Papi's head and whispered, "Thank you for coming," in perfect English. Next came the customary photo ops. The flashes from every conceivable camera blinded Papi as he continued to stand between the two newlyweds with a huge smile.

Finally, with no warning, the wedding was over; the group was thankful that this wedding lasted only one day. Wealthy Indian weddings can last as long as five days. As quickly as Papi could, he blessed the couple and retreated to the long-awaited air-conditioned car. Having thought ahead, Premdas had the car running, and it was already cooled down. Knowing the food would not be acceptable for the western stomach the group decided to eat at Prakash on their return to the campus. The sun was floating on the western horizon as the contented group returned to Prakash

This was not the end of the ceremonies for the very tired and hot young couple. There was one more compulsory ceremony for the girl's mother to gift five things to her daughter after the marriage: *taat* (plate), *gilas* (glass), *polltat* (wooden bread block), *belan* (rolling pin), *kadai* (wok). The program is called *bidaai*. It continued with the girl touching the feet of all the elderly people and saying goodbye to her family. Sheshi counseled herself not to cry. She was determined to show a happy countenance.

The wedding feast lasted until late in the night.

Then she and Vasentha went to his village. The marriage was finally irrevocable.

Chapter 27:
Reception

On Saturday the 22nd, a reception was held at Vasentha's village. Waiting for the day to cool somewhat, the wedding entourage from Prakash again persisted over furrowed, potholed roads and arrived at 5:00 p.m. to be greeted by about two hundred people. The girl's side selected people to come to the boy's village for the reception program. The ever-present gaggle of dirt-encrusted children with big, round brown eyes greeted the visitors. Mr. Vasentha . . . a married man now . . . welcomed Papi Sir with the now-traditional hug and marigold garland.

Papi could hardly contain his joy at seeing this young man happily married to a Christian girl.

Vasentha proudly insisted that Papi Sir see all the gifts they had received for their wedding. As tradition dictated, he and Sheshi would now share the family home with his newly married brother and his wife and his parents. The two small rooms would be overflowing with people.

Blue plastic tarps had been hung in a feeble attempt at a *pendahl*. The only thing it really accomplished was to cut the meager flow of air. There was one white plastic chair relegated to the center of the dirt enclosure for the honored guest. Both of the newly married couples stood behind Papi. Not wanting to be the center of attention, Papi tried unsuccessfully to stand in the back.

The Chief of the village came forward and welcomed Papi by saying, "We are happy you came for this program and wedding, even though it is so hot. We always learn something new from you when you come. We welcome you."

Dr. Suresh gave the two couples (Vasentha's brother was also married on the 21st of May and this was a common reception for both the couples) a few verses from the Bible.

> *Wives, submit to your own husbands, as to the Lord. For the husband is the head of the wife even as Christ is the head of the church, his body, and is himself its Savior. Now as the church submits to Christ, so also wives should submit in everything to their husbands.*
>
> *Husbands, love your wives, as Christ loved the church and gave himself up for her.*
> Ephesians 5: 22–25 (NIV)

He then asked Vasentha to open his Bible, and Vasentha said, "I don't have my Bible with me; my friend has taken it from me to read." Dr. Suresh was so joyful to know this. A new Bible had to be found for Vasentha.

Thankfully, Suresh's talk was short. Papi offered a prayer for both couples and surprised each of them with a monetary gift.

Vasentha was grinning from ear to ear. Papi thought, *WOW, he must be a very happy married man.* But just as these thoughts were rolling around in his head, a surprise program for him began. Papi had completed seventy years on the 13th of May and Vasentha had decided to celebrate Papi's birthday at his reception. He presented a card to Papi with a hand-painted, large yellow flower in the middle. This handcrafted card had seventy people's signatures or thumbprints on it . . . the oldest person was seventy-four years old and the youngest was six months.

Papi was overwhelmed with joy and surprise upon receiving such a thoughtful gift. He held it up for a

multitude of pictures. Then followed the "Happy Birthday" song in a complex tribal tune, but Papi said, "I don't know about the song, but I will clap to the beat." It was a short and extremely sweet ceremony.

Happily, it was not too much longer before Papi and the gang again retreated to the relief of the air-conditioned car.

After the foreign guests left, the entire village sat for the reception dinner. Roasted mutton and rice (an extremely rare treat) was served. Vasentha stood proudly with arms folded upon his chest . . . a stance that would become synonymous with his posture. He was proud that he could provide such a feast.

After the reception and dinner, the bride must then return to her village. This was a five-hour, arduous bus trip. *Paradhi* tribes have a special ceremony called *Satyanarayan pooja*. In this they worship *satyanaraya*n god. It is simply a formality to give permission to the newly married couple for their honeymoon. Only then can they start their own family life. With much fanfare, the groom then must travel separately to the village and bring his bride home.

Chapter 28:
Skype

Technology is a miracle that Nani has embraced wholeheartedly. There were times years ago when she would try to place a call to Papi in India and literally wait for hours . . . pushing redial . . . to get through to India. One distinct memory was of a night when, worn out from the hours of sitting by the home phone, she finally got an answer. "Hello, hello, is Mr. Loren there?" In very broken English, the housefather's wife said, "Five minutes; I go get him," and promptly hung up. Nani, exhausted, just sat there and cried. With resolve, she started the entire process over again, connecting with Papi in only a few tries. Needless to say, all staff was then instructed to *never* hang up on a call for Mr. Loren. In India you must learn patience.

Email used to drop the connection with regularity. Sending to more than a very small group was impossible. Now, though the Internet service was completely overloaded and affected by regular power outages, emails were the mainstay for communication.

Then Skype came on the scene. Oh, how Nani loved this new technology. Even though there was a time-zone difference of nine and a half hours (sometimes ten and a half), the ability to see Papi's smiling face helped with the loneliness.

On the wedding trip for Vasentha's wedding, it was arranged for Papi to go to Vasentha's village after the marriage and try to Skype. The appointed time arrived and, with computer in hand, the ensemble from Prakash headed again to ride over the rough, rutted trek to the distant village. Women carrying huge bundles of firewood toiled along the narrow paths, bent under the weight of the burdens, sharing reluctantly the meager roadway with the foreigner's vehicle.

When the path narrowed, making it impossible for the car to continue, the individuals exited the car and were escorted to Vasentha's hut. In the space in front of a few huts, chickens clucked and scratched. Children ran alongside, hands outstretched with the knowledge that Papi would have chocolates in his pocket. Do a thing one time and it becomes a tradition in India. Each trip to this village amazed Papi as he saw people living the way they have lived throughout the history of the world. As Thomas Hoover wrote in his novel *The Moghul*, "Most Indians think everything they have and everything they do is absolutely perfect, exactly the way it is. They might take something foreign and use it, or copy it but they always have to appear disdainful of anything not Indian."

Time was taken to try to explain what was about to transpire. Papi used an orange to explain, "The earth is round like this orange. Nani is here and we are here." The heads wiggled from side to side, which is the normal acknowledgement of hearing, but does not mean there is a true understanding.

Papi sat on a small cot and opened the silver computer with the Apple insignia. All of the huge brown eyes stared at the magical contraption. The Chief, with all his authority, placed his chair directly in front of Papi. With feet together and hands folded neatly in his lap, the Chief, dressed in his finest (brown leather hat, white neatly pressed shirt, and black trousers) waited for the auspicious ceremony to begin.

Zing-beep, zing-beep . . . the very distinctive ring of Skype began. Papi turned the computer and there was Nani's face in living color on the screen. She excitedly said, "Hi everyone. It is so very nice to see you all. It is worth staying up so late." Actually, all she could really see was the Chief's upper body consuming the entire screen.

"Chief, you are looking very handsome." Dr. Suresh giggled as he translated this comment. The dark face of the Chief remained stoic.

"Loren, I want to see the new bride," said Nani. As Papi turned the computer screen toward the young couple, all Nani could see was the body of the Chief slowly leaning as he tried to stay in the picture. She got so tickled that the conversation had to cease till she could restore her dignity. Finally, Papi realized the problem and brought the young newlyweds to the forefront. Shyness overtook the young couple and they would not look into the camera. Even so, the whole experiment was worth the effort.

Later, in a phone conversation, Papi and Nani discussed what on earth these dear, deprived people could be thinking. They asked themselves, how as Americans can we relate to this encounter? If we were placed on the moon tomorrow, we would still be more prepared for the experience. Our three-year-olds know more about technology than these villagers.

Still, Nani could only say, "God Bless Niklas and Janus, who invented Skype in 2003."

Chapter 29:
Translation

At the request of the village Chief, Vasentha and Sheshi started the translation of the book of John into the *Paradhi* language. Since *Paradhi* has no alphabet or written language, they used the *Marathi* alphabet, but the tonal sounds would be different. This would also allow Dr. Suresh and Nupi to put the manuscript into the computer so it could be published.

"Vasentha, do not be so lazy," bemoaned Sheshi. No well-intentioned words from her could move him  one minute faster. She was much more organized and wanted more committed time from her husband. He read the *Marathi* and she wrote in the large notebook the *Paradhi* words.

There was the potential of reaching fourteen thousand people in the surrounding villages with the good news of *Yeshu*. Vasentha had oh-so-willingly taken the task of handwriting the translation and the Prakash staff would put each precious word into the computer at the Institutes.

Some of the people had already requested the New Testament in *Marathi* so they could try to read what was written. Most often it was the children now attending school that would read the stories in the evenings to the family.

Chapter 30:
Baby Loren

Visiting Vasentha's village was on the agenda for each of Papi and Nani's visits to India. There were times of tremendous unrest when a visit was quite impossible, but today they were able to make the arduous trip on the bumpy, uneven roads into the jungle.

It was a peaceful scene from another age . . . in striking contrast to their first encounter with this dirty, desolate village.

After a sweet and informative visit, Nani was getting ready to return to the car when she said, "Vasentha, I saw the notebooks you wrote as a translation of the book of John. It is beautifully done."

He said, "My wife did the writing. She is here to see YOU."

What? She was pregnant and was supposedly two hundred kilometers away with her mother. The custom in India is that daughters stay with their mothers during pregnancy. By tradition, a pregnant woman always moves back into her family home from

126

three months before the birth of the child until three months after the birth.

Nani was so shocked that she turned, ran, and hugged the girl . . . to Sheshi's utter embarrassment. It is so typical of God, who delights in doing things in ways we would never dream of, to make sure Nani was able to see her and compliment her.

She was definitely pregnant and so very shy. This had to have been a difficult trip and was certainly completely out of the norm.

On Tuesday, April 3, 2012, Mr. and Mrs. Vasentha were blessed with a baby boy. Usually the father is not allowed to see the baby for at least a month.

Vasentha could hardly contain his excitement as he rode the big red government bus to Sheshi's village. He was able to find a seat when he first entered, but very soon was sharing it with four other people. The seats are made for two people. His thoughts whirled as he thought of being a new father. His own father was not an example of what he wanted for his children. With a wheeze and a hiss, the bus finally stopped in the small village and the people piled out.

Vasentha knew he was breaking tradition by arriving early to gather his wife and child before the month's end. Standing tall as he sauntered toward Sheshi's family home, he saw Sheshi, with the tiny babe, his eyes lined with the black *kohl* to keep the evil spirits away, on her hip, waiting expectantly in the *zhopadi* doorway. Without warning, a smile creased his normally sober face.

I'm a father, he thought.

Feeling awkward, but still wanting to touch the baby, Vasentha stretched out his arms to hold the wee child. Large brown eyes stared up at him with complete confidence. Oh . . . the responsibility hit him like a ton of bricks. Love came effortlessly. He planned to show more affection than was culturally the norm. *Dr. Suresh hugs and shows his love to his daughters. I can do the same. It is a good thing.*

The bus ride back to their village seemed to Vasentha to be much less strenuous. He was not concerned with getting home as much as with the welfare of his wife and new baby. His puffed chest was a sure sign of a new father . . . and it was not just a child—it was a BOY. Some cultures will not even acknowledge a girl child as part of the family.

The evening sky was washed in the copper light of the setting sun as the very tired but happy threesome entered the village.

A few days after the arrival of the new babe, the "*Naming Ceremony Program*" was to take place. Because the child was a boy, every older woman in the village and surrounding villages was automatically a part of the festivities. Each woman had a perfect suggestion for *best name*.

Sheshi and Vasentha arrived with the babe swaddled in pink. There was no distinction of gender from the color of clothing. They were just thankful to have such a beautiful outfit. The young mother had dutifully stirred the black powder into a paste and carefully applied it to the babe's forehead and around his eyes. This was to keep the evil spirits away. She would not have dared to arrive at the revels without this black decoration. Vasentha and she were both followers of *Yeshu*, but they still would follow some of the customs of the tribe. Customs and religion are intricately intertwined in all of Indian societies.

Taking their seats in the center of the group, the young family quietly and carefully listened to each woman's suggestion for the *best name*, but when the actual time came, Sheshi stood . . . her heart pounding and pounding . . . and said, "I want the baby's name to be Loren. I like the real Loren Sir. He is a loving and beautiful gentleman. I want our son to be educated and caring like Loren Papi." So her mother-in-law, as the authority, declared Loren the *best name* for the baby. Everyone accepted that as the *BEST name* for the baby.

With bravery unfelt before, the young couple stood and said, "We want to give a hearty thanks to *Yeshu* for this special gift of a son. We want to educate our son so that he will do some good work for our tribe."

Then the entire village had a meal together and celebrated the new inductee into the village. As they ate, gifts were given. Nani had sent hand-stitched cloth napkins (diapers) made for the new baby knowing that they would be used only occasionally. Sheshi and Vasentha opened the beautifully wrapped package and smiled at the totally American gift.

Chapter 31:
Baptism

For several months, Vasentha had felt a hunger in his heart to be baptized. Boldly, he approached Dr. Suresh and said, "Why are you not baptizing me? I trust that *Yeshu* is my Savior. He is my Lord."

This was not the first time Vasentha had asked about baptism. Dr. Suresh was reluctant only because the culture of Christianity in India makes baptism be an automatic membership in a local church. Not being a reverend, Dr. Suresh knew he would have to have one of the local pastors with him at the time of the baptism. There was no way he wanted Vasentha bound to a local church. Stealing of others' ministries is not uncommon in India, and there was still too much uncertainty in the *Paradhi* village to have interference by an outside pastor.

Also, the laws of India have mandatory registration of conversion with the police department. So it required a licensed reverend to sign the papers of baptism. Again, the freedom of religion guaranteed by the India Constitution is very encumbered.

Dr. Suresh mulled over in his mind how he would handle this delicate situation. "I think I will enlist the help of my brother-in-law, Nagesh," he said to Nupi. "I can tell him issues outright and he will not then expect Vasentha to be a member of his church in the city."

"Hey, Nagesh. This is Suresh. I have huge request to make you. You know the *Paradhi* village I have been working in for past eighteen years? Well, one of the young men wants to be baptized. I need you to help me, but he cannot become a member of your church. I know this is the custom, but it just cannot happen."

There was no hesitation in Nagesh's affirmative response. "But, Suresh, where will this baptism take place? I hope not in that lake with so much mud and sewage? It will be very difficult to stand. Giving baptism to this boy will not be pleasing experience because of the stinky, muddy water, but from God's point of view, I think it is perfect."

The very next Saturday was set as the day for the joyful event. Vasentha arose earlier than normal due to his excitement. First and foremost, he had a meeting set with the Chief. Over the last few days, when he realized the baptism was actually going to take place, he had some fear about telling his village and the Chief that he was going to be baptized. As he sat waiting for the Chief to arrive, he prayed, "*Yeshu*, let these people see you in me."

Expecting a plethora of problems, Vasentha had tea ready to be served for the Chief's arrival. Cautiously, he said, "Sir, I wanted to let you know that I plan to be baptized as a Christian today. I hope you will not deny me this opportunity."

The Chief, not even taking time to mull it over, said, "Vasentha, you have lived a good life. You are an example to all of us. If this is your desire, no one will deny you." With a loud gush of air, Vasentha let out the breath he had been holding.

While traveling to the lake, fear muted Vasentha's enthusiasm. Following *Yeshu* had its complications. A myriad of thoughts swarmed his head. How would his simple village-boy life change? Would he still be accepted in the village? Would the police become a nuisance? The power to choose one's fate was the entitlement of the prosperous, not a village boy.

Joy filled his young heart as he arrived at the lake to find a large group of people waiting. *They really love me to make such an effort on this scorching-hot, humid day.*

Next to no flesh between his skin and bones was evident as Vasentha started to remove his clothing. Then, seeing Dr. Suresh was not removing his clothing, he, with a very la-di-dah gait belying his nervousness, walked toward the lake, not even noticing the sewage mixed with muddy-water runoff that formed the lake.

Nagesh and Suresh looked at each other wondering if they were fools to take such a huge chance of disease by entering the filthy lake. Normally, they would not have put their big toes in this contaminated water, but this was for Vasentha.

This place is so much of mud; it was difficult to stand in the water. Many times I lost my balance just trying to walk in. It was muddy water, but this boy was looking very excited for taking baptism, thought Nagesh.

He swallowed back a spike of acid burning up his throat. Not wanting to prolong their stay in the mucky waters, Nagesh got to the point rather quickly. "Vasentha, do you believe that Jesus is your Lord and Savior? Have you accepted him  and intend to live your life as a Christ follower?" The gathering fell so silent you could almost hear the grass growing.

All could hear a resounding, *"HO."*

"Then, because of your profession of faith in *Yeshu* as your personal Savior, and by the power vested in me by the State Government of India, I now baptize you in the name of the Father, the Son, and the Holy Spirit. Amen."

As the slimy water flooded over his head and body, Vasentha felt the unbelievable power of *Yeshu*. He rose out of the water with hands in the air, shouting, "*Devanu jayjaykar ho*, praise God." The blue sky brightened around him, and mucky water seemed to sparkle. A slice of heaven for him.

The afore silent group of spectators broke into resounding applause.

Nagesh and Suresh could not exit the scummy waters fast enough. The moisture—the fetal matter mixed with water runoff—clung to their bodies.

Both their wives stood with soapy rags for them to wash their arms and legs. Still, even with all the smell and aggravation of the lake, they felt exhilarated.

Shyly, Vasentha took the hands of Dr. Suresh and Nagesh and said, "*Dhanyawad, dhanyawad*, thank you. Please come to my house for tea."

Vasentha wished his wife and baby son could have seen his life-changing experience. He had shown the world he was a *Yeshu* follower. The heat of the afternoon sun dried his wet clothing in no time.

In his mind he had planned to walk back to his village, but Dr. Suresh said, "Vasentha, let me take you on the motorcycle, and we can tell the Chief and your wife about today's events. Nagesh and the others will follow. We will celebrate your special day."

As they were riding toward the village, the sky was washed in the reddish-brown light of the setting sun. *What a day*, thought Vasentha, *I was almost beginning to think it would never happen.*

Entering the village, Vasentha realized the entire community was sitting awaiting his arrival. They wanted to hear every detail of the "baptism experience." Vasentha knew God's timing was perfect. Now the villagers were ready to hear the story of *Yeshu*.

Again, *Devanu jayjaykar ho*, praise God.

Chapter 32:
Medical Camp

Vasentha woke just as streaks of orange and pink splashed the morning sky. He stretched and walked out of the *zhopadi* knowing that this was an auspicious day for his village. Reluctantly, the heads had agreed to let Dr. Suresh bring four white guests (Nani, Papi and Nani's sister and brother-in-law) and other doctors to their village for a medical camp. Vasentha was not sure exactly what that was. Dr. Suresh was a doctor for animals, not humans, but he had assured the heads that the villagers would be happy with the camp. Outsiders were not normally welcomed in the village, but it was evident that the love connection with Dr. Suresh was there and the "*Prakash*" light of *Yeshu* showed through, even amid tremendous poverty.

Vasentha counted on his fingers to remember all the things that still needed to be done before the guests arrived. The large, multi-colored cloth *pendahl* was erected and the green fake grass had been laid.

Now he just needed to put up the metal tables they had rented for the occasion.

For the umpteenth time, the rambunctious kids ran to him and asked when *Saheb* Papi and the guests would arrive. The very first thing on the list was that he must round up chairs for all the guests. He would just invade each *zhopadi* and confiscate the precious possessions.

"Sheshi, I need for you to go buy eight garlands. Don't get tiny, skimpy ones but big, nice ones. Our guests today are very special."

Papi and Nani could hardly contain their excitement, but some fear niggled at their thoughts. Years of ministry could be destroyed through no fault of their own; by taking unwanted pictures, or entering a sacred place without permission, the new guests could offend the heads.

As they all sat at breakfast, Nani said, "Hey, sister, I need to go over some of the do's and don'ts for today. You and Ron need to be very conscious of the fact that these people have never allowed outsiders into their village, so no pictures unless you ask permission. (Verna's camera was an appendage to her arm.) Even if you see or smell something disgusting, please do not react. They will be all too aware of your body language. You cannot go gadding about without one of us. You must not eat anything in the village. This is not an option. They will offer you tea or a *chapatti*, but politely say no even though it will smell great. We want you to enjoy your day, but it is a priority not to offend."

"Well, all right, so we will just follow your lead," Verna said less than enthusiastically. She could barely sit still from anticipation. Ron sat with the expression he customarily wore: lips turned upward with a hint of a smile. His medical background had him in high anticipation of the coming day.

Loading the *Qualis* took some concerted effort . . . lunches, pre-made tea with use-and-throw cups, supplies for the doctors had to be loaded before the eight passengers could cram themselves into the overloaded vehicle.

"*Jaldi, jaldi,* Sunil, we need to get the lunch box in the back first," encouraged Nani. The guest cook scampered to do her bidding.

Due to his height (over six feet), Ron sat in the front seat with Premdas, the driver, and had one throat-closing, stomach-grinding moment when the car nearly collided with a large rattling bullock cart that decided the road was his to cross. "Hey, Ron, did you put a hole in my car's floorboard?" Papi teased laughingly.

Having just arrived in India and been introduced to only the beauty and the wealthier side of the country, Ron and Verna were appalled to see the villagers dwelling in decrepit mud-brick homes. The thatched roof of one hovel was completely caved in, but the inhabitants still were residing inside. The deeper the octet drove into the jungle, the more pungent smells of unkempt humanity began to assault the senses of those unaccustomed to unwashed bodies and dung-fueled fires. Filth, odors, and disease-infected villages were along each side of the rough track. Scruffy children ran to see the unusual vehicle.

Verna's sensitive nature was overwhelmed. Tears ran uninhibited down her cheeks. "Oh, Nani, this is so sad. How do you stand to see this poverty all the time?"

Nani replied, "We do for one what we wish we could do for all. You will see the difference Vasentha has made in his village."

Still not sure this experiment of allowing other outsiders into Vasentha's village was a good idea, Papi asked that all the vehicle's occupants remain inside until he could assess the situation. The large, colorful *pendahl* was not in view from where the car was parked, so the village looked deserted. Verna's camera was clicking a mile a minute. Anxious to get out and explore, they felt that the short wait seemed like hours. Finally, Papi returned with Vasentha and the procession of white foreigners started through the never-ending sea of people. Again, the dissimilarity to the previous villages was stark.

Unseen until now, shy women stood in doorways and whispered behind their hands and nudged one another. The guests' nostrils were assailed by the redolence of curry and spices that emanated from the huts, such a change from the overwhelming pongs they had just encountered. Still, each step had to

be carefully navigated down the rutted pathway. The contrast of neat brick-and-mud homes with tile roofs was extremely evident to each beholder.

Eventually, the assemblage rounded the corner and the beautifully decorated *pendahl* came into view. The multi-colored fabric laced to bamboo poles seemed an unobtainable feat for such a poverty-stricken village. Having never seen the decorative tents so prevalent in India for special events, Verna and Ron stood in awe. *"How do they do it?"* is always the question. The camera continued to *click* with unending rhythm. As far as Papi and Nani could see, she had neglected to ask permission, but no one seemed to mind.

There, hanging in a most prominent place, was an enormous banner: "Vet-Med Medical Camp." Hordes of people suffering from protein deficiencies and malnutrition were already lined up for the first-time experience of having a doctor examine them.

But, as is the custom, the necessary "tea ceremony and garland giving" had to take place before any examinations could begin.

Vasentha, with chest puffed out in pride, ushered forward the reluctant . . . but eager . . . young girls who bore the elaborate garlands for each of the honored foreign guests. Handing her camera to Dr. Suresh, Verna posed with head bent and received her floral offering. Loud applause was given after each garland was placed over the head of the visitor. As was the tradition with Papi, he immediately took his garland off and placed it over Nani's head . . . this provoked a thunderous handclapping and whistling. This distinct honor was rarely seen.

Thankfully, sufficient use-and-throw cups had been brought and plenty of the sugary tea to delight all the dignitaries in attendance. *Click. Click. Click.*

Pictures were taken for verification of sure-to-be long-lasting memories.

Nupi and Premdas took up their positions at the assembled tables to begin taking the vitals of each person seeking medical attention. There was a bathroom scale to weigh every patient. Having never seen such a contraption, some villagers were reluctant to stand on this thing. Nupi, with her soft-spoken way, encouraged each to stand and be weighed. She also asked each person his or her age. Most had no idea.

One lady said, "Can't that thing there tell you?" pointing to the scale. This initiated a belly laugh from all within hearing.

Ron was intrigued by the methods used by the visiting doctors taking blood pressures and blood-sugar levels. These are the most common problems of the Indians. Since it became popular to eat wheat *chapattis* instead of *jowar roti* with the customary cup of sugared tea, sugar diabetes has run rampant. The ratio of carbohydrates and protein due to the sugar wheat educes is completely out of sync now with this change of diet. The technique used was more the ancient art of acupuncture. The pressure points of each patient were poked and prodded. Beads were placed on relevant spots. The villagers obtaining these tiny artifacts treasured them as if they were sent from the gods. *Click. Click. Click.* They showed off their treasures for the camera.

Just for the fun of it, Premdas stood in the long line to have his blood pressure taken. It was over-the-top high. Then he was not sure if he had done the correct thing . . . ignorance was bliss. On the way home Papi and Nani suggested he go to his regular physician for a real check-up, only to find that he had none.

As lunchtime approached, smoke from the dung-fueled fires began to fill the air. With smiling faces, offers of *chapattis* were given as the camera continued to *click*.

"Oh, yummy," said Verna.

"No, you cannot eat them, Verna, even though they smell wonderful."

"Okay! I get it!"

Suddenly and without warning it began to pour. Before the team could reach the car, the water was ankle deep in some areas. Floating in the rivulets was every sort of disgusting debris. The pungent smell of fresh fecal matter accosted their nostrils.

"Eeewwww, disgusting!"

The retreat could not be fast enough. Not falling was of upmost importance. Just imagining the junk in the water on their white faces was sufficient incentive to keep them upright.

The sanitary wipes were out in abundance for the waterlogged feet. Then little by little giggles erupted into full-fledged laughter. Memory-making at its worst.

Making their way back to the main road would be considered an act of heroism by most. The wipers swished away the watery curtain. Every small gully was flooded and the ruts and potholes were obscured by flowing water. Papi instructed Premdas to drive with extra care. Because the rain overshadowed their plans for a picnic lunch in the jungle, the ensemble decided to go to a friend's farm and use his upstairs apartment facilities.

Click. Click. Click. Every moment would be recorded for posterity. Relationship-building was one of Dr. Suresh's fortes, and because of his Self-Reliant Training, use of the home's conveniences gave the team a delightful and clean rest stop.

Thankfully, the rain stopped and the group was able to trek the muddy path into the orange groves. By climbing the trees, they were able to gather bags full of the delicious orange-and-green fruit that had made Nagpur famous. Nagpur oranges have a distinctive orange-green coloring unlike American store-bought oranges.

Chapter 33:
Returning to Old Village
With the Gospel

Vasentha began to have a burden in his heart for the people of his old village. Since the translating of the book of John, he felt the need to tell the village of his childhood about *Yeshu*.

The kids he had done Sunday school with and the Pot program performance as a boy were grown and now mothers and fathers like him. Since he had left, no one had entered the village with any kind of Christian teaching. This head was so angry that Vasentha had vacated the village that he would not allow even Dr. Suresh to enter the vicinity.

Vasentha and Sheshi prayed that if Vasentha made the approximately twenty-four-kilometer walk to the old village, he would be accepted without harm.

Streaks of orange and pink splashed the morning sky in a welcoming design as Vasentha walked out of his hut to greet the new day. With each stride, he asked *Yeshu* for protection and for words that would convince the head of his good intentions. Because the head continued to be so angry about Vasentha moving out of the village, it was quite possible the head would do him bodily harm if he again entered the village. *Yeshu* must prepare the heart of the head. No contact had been made since Vasentha's departure.

Vasentha decided that if he were greeted with no hostility, he would just ask to have a Children's Club. The head just might be more accepting of a club than a Sunday school.

Vasentha thought of the many ways he could help the total lifestyle of these children in fun and interesting ways. He had such fond memories of how Dr. Suresh and Madam Nupi had taught him. It brought a smile to his face as he remembered that first haircut and bath. He had been so sure the cutting of the hair was going to hurt. He had not realized at the time that this event would be investing in future laughter.

As he walked, the sun not yet a scorching heat overhead, he stopped for a much-needed drink of water. He had learned from Dr. Suresh years ago to never start a trek without the life-saving liquid. He continued to ask *Yeshu* for inspiration about the new venture.

Uncertainty and fear niggled at his thoughts. *Maybe the walk was so long because this adventure needed to be bathed in more prayer?*

So deep in his thoughts, Vasentha was surprised when he finally focused and saw the chosen village just on the horizon. He had truly forgotten how very desolate were the surroundings of this village.

He was all too aware that if the head did not accept him, the villagers could stone him or beat him without mercy. So with shoulders held back and the gait of a confident villager, Vasentha entered the mishmash of crumbling brick-and-thatched *zhopadis.*

The jealousy once held by the now-folically challenged head had completely disappeared and Vasentha was welcomed with a wide grin. Vasentha had to mentally command his legs to move. He thought, *why should I be shocked by this warm reception? Was this not exactly what I have been praying for on the long trek?* Why are we surprised when *Yeshu* answers our prayers?

After he was ushered into the head's *zhopadi,* the ceremonial tea was prepared. Having now learned the value of filtered and pure water, Vasentha started to refuse the tin cup of hot, steaming tea. Then, with a quick prayer for being stupid, he accepted the small cup with gratitude.

He scratched his dusty face with his free hand. "I wish to start a Children's Club here in your village," began Vasentha. "I want to teach new life skills to the village children and, with your permission, get them ready to go to school." The silence was oppressive as he waited for the head's reply. Eager to make his case for the validity of this program, Vasentha continued on, only to have the head stop him with a commanding lift of his hand.

"There is no need to try and convince me, Vasentha," said the head. "I have been observing the changes YOU"—he pointed his skinny finger in Vasentha's direction—"have made in your new village. We will welcome the help you can provide our children. When can you start this unique program?" Vasentha was overwhelmed and unprepared for this extremely positive dialogue.

"Well . . . errr . . . I will have to consult my wife and schedule with Dr. Suresh, but I assure you it will not be long from now."

It seemed as if he was walking on clouds as he went home. This was a faith-growing day he would never forget. *Devanu jayjaykar ho,* praise God!

The onerous thoughts were gone and life seemed to be heading in such a superior direction as Vasentha entered his village, only to again hear a violent squabble between his wife and his sister-in-law. This was the umpteenth time this had happened.

"Why today, Yeshu, *when everything has been so wonderful?"*

Chapter 34:
Our New Home

Entering the village after a long day herding the goats in the jungle (he no longer gathered the bright-yellow berries used for the winemaking,) Vasentha was exhausted, his body streaked with sweat and grime.

Hearing the quarreling from inside his humble home, a frown was brought to his mocha-colored forehead. *This is not a good thing.* Yeshu *would not approve of my wife's bickering with her sister-in law. They will never see the love of* Yeshu *with this behavior. What must I do?*

His brooding mood was very apparent to Sheshi. *What can be troubling my husband?* she wondered. *Life is not good, even in this nice house, with its fiery barbs coming from every direction. Life would be better alone.*

Exhausted after his day's work, Vasentha entered the *zhopadi* and lay down on the cot in his portion of the family home. Looking around the brightly painted room, his eyes fell to the shelf his mother had containing all the icons of the village gods—a rock, a piece of decorative glass, a portion of burled wood, and a photo. Being animistic in belief, the villagers think everything in nature has a soul and, therefore, collects objects of interest as a god. Again, a frown creased his forehead. *Do I want all these gods displayed in my home,* he thought?

As he had stopped doing winemaking and help to his parents with shared income, ultimately the load of income for the parents came upon his brother. So this was why the two daughters-in-law were quarreling. The father, being a drunkard, had not shared in the family income since Vasentha was a small child and was a bird-catcher.

It was the custom in the village that upon marriage, most of the married couples would feel comfortable going out and staying in their own homes. Vasentha's brother would continue living in the family home, but Vasentha would still hold equal rights. He assumed from earlier conversations that his mother also thought it was good for them to stay away, as she didn't want any quarrels in the village.

Trying to alleviate any further trouble in a not-so-classic, spur-of-the-moment decision, Vasentha said, "We will build our own house."

Oops. What just came out of my mouth? reflected Vasentha. This was a quick decision, but the implementation would not be easy. The Chief owned, or so he claimed, all the land of the village. In all actuality, the villagers were squatters on government land.

He felt a sweat start to pour off him as he thought of asking the Chief for land for a new home.

He did not feel completely courageous as he, in his swaying gait, walked to the Chief's front veranda. The Chief's home stood out as the most elaborate of the village. His dwelling was the be-all and end-all of existence in a village. No one would dare to outdo the Chief. With hesitation, he rapped at the door. Vasentha was pleased when the Chief's wife opened the door, her skin crinkled over pointy bones, but her smile warm.

"May I please speak with the Chief on a most personal matter?"

"He is eating his meal. Let me ask if he will talk to you now."

Vasentha stood with arms crossed over his chest; his pulse throbbed in his throat.

He would not have to wait long; the Chief's respect for Vasentha was evident in his quick appearance. Usually, the Chief would have finished his mid-day meal and might have taken a nap before making his appearance to an uninvited guest.

Vasentha sat and began to explain his dilemma. Without hesitation, the Chief gave him a new plot across the gully from the village. He said, "I also find it is better to move out than further quarrel. I am not upset over this matter, as it is your family matter."

Sheshi and Vasentha began to gather sticks and brush from the nearby jungle. Laboring as day passed into night, light swallowed by darkness, the young couple toiled to build a new home.

Sheshi meticulously labored, her *sari* covering her head, with the cow-dung and water to smooth the ground to a glossy surface where the hut would be built. The sun, a fiery untamed ball, burned Vasentha's shoulders, unprotected by his torn shirt, as he labored beside her.

Now they could begin to drive the *saboble* poles into the ground and weave the twigs and grasses making a wall of brush. Vasentha knew he needed to make the structure large enough to house not only his family, but also his herd of twelve goats. Sheshi would never live with the goats invading her living space. As it was, the baby kids would wiggle their way into the living space.

Even as industriously as the young couple had worked, light filtered through the canopy of leaves, brush, and twigs that made up the roof of the *zhopadi*. Vasentha recognized this was not an option; he must go into Nagpur city and sell one of his precious goats in order to buy a blue tarp for the roof. Monsoon would arrive in no time and without the tarp, it would be impossible to live with a baby in the meager *zhopadi*.

Going into the city would require the motorcycle. While living in the family home, there was no issue with its use, but the motorcycle belonged to his father, because he paid the seed money and paid the entire loan. Now Vasentha felt he needed to ask permission. Would his father be sober enough to even make a decision?

This was so not—or—one bit anything he ever wanted to do, but he had no choice. Carrying the goat in his arms to the city was not a possibility either.

Finding his father smack-dab in the middle of the path, drunk and disheveled in his filthy garb, was not surprising. Gently, Vasentha raised his father from the dung-infested ground and led him to the family home. As he laid him on the cot inside, he asked, "Father, may I use the motorcycle to take my goat to the city to sell?" The teachings of *Yeshu* said to respect your father and mother . . . no matter what. His father grumbled, "*Tikai, tikai . . .*" (Okay, okay, be gone.)

As he arrived at the marketplace, Vasentha blinked the dust of a Nagpur May out of his eyes. A savvier negotiator was never born than Vasentha, but even he stood gape-mouthed as the auctioneer announced the price he would receive for his female goat. Now he could purchase a humongous blue tarp for his roof.

At long last, it was the day of the move. It would take very few trips to transport their scanty belongings across the gully to the new home.

Sheshi and Vasentha, with baby Loren, sat outside, silent while bugs, attracted by the single bulb, whirred in the night. Their home was finished. Led by the same desire, silently they rose and went into the hut and knelt on the floor of cow-dung and beaten earth, by the single cot, and gave thanks to *Yeshu*.

Chapter 35:
Appointment

Vasentha was relaxing in the shade of the only tree in the village when he saw Dr. Suresh arrive. This was nothing out of the ordinary, so he was not in the least prepared for the extraordinary outcome of the day.

Thankfully, it was not his day to take all the village goats to the jungle to graze. Seeing the success that Vasentha was having economically with his goats, several of the other young men had petitioned the government, with Dr. Suresh's help, for a pair of goats.

Now the village boasted a herd of thirty-eight goats, and winemaking was no longer the sole income of the village. The young men decided that it was not necessary for all of them to go the jungle every day. Dividing the responsibilities gave each man more free time. Vasentha used his free time to make sure the twenty-six children he had encouraged to go to school were actually prepared to attend—bathed, clothes clean, hair combed, and homework completed. Brushing the teeth was not yet a part of the daily routine.

Dr. Suresh stood at the entrance of the small "courtyard" Vasentha had incorporated onto his hut. This gave a place for his school kids to meet and a place for Baby Loren to play.

"*Aajao*, Vasentha. Please come. I have important issue to discuss with you."

Vasentha jumped up and ran . . . not his customary gait . . . to meet the good doctor, questions niggling at his thoughts. *What could be so important?*

As they walked, Dr. Suresh said, "I have just met with Papi, and as executive director of Prakash for India, we have a once-in-a-lifetime unimaginable opportunity to present to you."

Vasentha held his breath. "What is an opportunity?" he shyly asked.

"Oh, I'm so sorry. It is an appointment to a post as my assistant. We agreed that you and Sheshi, too, have done an exceptional job with the children of this village. First, we want you to continue this work, but also we want you to continue to go to your old village and work more often with the children there. Would you be willing to accept this responsibility?"

It didn't take Vasentha a nanosecond to mull it over. "HO, HO. We knew *Yeshu* had a job for us."

Dr. Suresh was pleasantly surprised at his quick answer without a word about *rupees*.

"Of course, this would be a paid position."

Vasentha's face lit up with a rare smile, not the expression he customarily wore. "*Ahcha*, I understand. *Dhanyawad*."

Vasentha and Sheshi took on the challenge with gusto uncommon to the *Paradhis*. The village life is exceedingly undisciplined and unstructured. The couple started by making a regular time of rising in the mornings and even made a list of their obligations. To them it seemed like a never-ending sea of duties.

After two or three visits, walking the twenty-four kilometers to the old village, Sheshi became concerned about the transportation. She did not have the stamina of her husband.

"Vasentha, I think we must pray about getting bicycle. That is good . . . right?"

Such a grand prayer, would Yeshu *actually hear*? he thought. Not wanting to let Sheshi know his true doubt, he answered in the one-syllable affirmative, "*HO.*"

Yeshu answered the prayer and more . . . yet another miracle in the life of Vasentha.

Not more than two weeks later, Papi and Nani arrived at the village. Papi was on the motorcycle with Dr. Suresh and Nani followed in a car.

Oh my. We must gather the children so they can sing the new songs, Vasentha thought as the visitors oohed and awed over his new home.

Nani giggled as she watched the entire group of children rise to sing with their arms crossed over across their chests . . . an exact replication of Vasentha's stanza. *It just shows how every little thing you do is watched and duplicated by the observant children,* she reflected.

She wiped the laughter tears from her eyes as the singing continued with each child to his or her own cadence.

The darling, wide-eyed boy in the front row caught her attention. *Could that be Connor?* At the end of the program, she asked Nupi to bring Connor to her. Indeed, it was the lad she had been drawn to.

How very serendipitous for my attention to be drawn to this child when this is a day of honoring our Connor.

At the end of the program, Papi made a pretense of wanting to see Vasentha and Sheshi's new home. He asked, "May we see inside?" He actually wanted to talk alone with the young couple.

When Nani and Papi's grandson Connor died from just one hit of Spice, many of their friends donated to Prakash for India. Connor had been part of a team that visited the institutes, and he began to feel he would someday take over Papi's position. It was decided that the funds given would honor him by buying a new, beautiful blue (Connor's favorite color) motorcycle for Dr. Suresh and refurbishing the old one for Vasentha. Connor loved to ride motorcycles and would have been pleased with this choice.

As Nani sat on the cow-dung floor, Papi sat the young on the small wooden cot just as a baby kid wormed his way through the brush and twig divider wall. Laughter erupted.

Vasentha was relieved. Papi seemed so serious. *What could be the problem?*

Papi stood in front of the couple and began by saying; "I know we have asked a lot of you by having you travel so far for ministry. We want to go where God is working and . . ."

Dr. Suresh touched Papi's arm. "Please, wait. I need to translate." Papi grinned and Vasentha expelled a breath held much too long. Papi realized he was sounding harsh, so he sat down between the two and continued, "Therefore, we want to give you Dr. Suresh's old motorcycle."

Vasentha jumped up, arms in the air. "*Devanu jayjaykar ho*, praise God."

Sheshi shyly said, "We have been praying for a bicycle. Never think such big thing come to us."

Then the truth was discovered. Vasentha had been riding his father's motorcycle for years without a proper license. Papi insisted he go for the license before he could take possession of the miracle gift, the be-all and end-all of luxury.

Chapter 36:
They Call Me "Sir"

The government offered a "scheme" of selling broken and half-bricks to the *Paradhi* villagers at a very reduced price. So the landscape of the village began to change as brick and cow-dung mud huts began to replace the stick-thatch *zhopadis*. No longer were there the odors, refuse, and disease that once filled the village because of Vasentha's work.

The noticeable changes did not include the potholed trace to the village. It still caused Nani to be white-knuckled on each trip.

Again, loaded down with tea jugs and use-and-throw cups, the ensemble from Prakash made the trek to the village to see Vasentha and Sheshi's new baby girl. Never to be without incident, there was a throat-closing, stomach-grinding moment when a young boy on a bicycle fell directly in front of the vehicle. Without the quick response by Premdas, the driver, the boy would have been crushed. As it was, he jumped up and, with a smile, went on his merry way.

By the time the group arrived at the village, Nani was ready for that ever-sweet cup of tea. Much of the fanfare was dispensed with now. Nani and Papi were family.

As everyone was finding a place and the adults and children were packing into the tiny hut, Nupi handed Nani a half-filled cup of tea. "Eeewwww, disgusting!" came out of Nani's mouth before she even realized it. *Sweet* was the understatement of the year. Nupi quickly took the cup and reassigned the precious liquid to another.

During the teatime, questions and answers were given as to the progress of Vasentha's "assignment."

He had twenty-six youngsters in his village that he helped each day and thirteen in his old village that were attending his Children's Club on a regular basis.

Vasentha stood with the expression he customarily wore and said, "Dr. Suresh, sir, tell Nani we want her to name our new baby girl." As the translation was going on, the baby, wet bottom and all, was handed to Nani. A diaper had been put on the infant in consideration of Nani, but was squishy wet. *Oh well, the hand can be washed,* thought Nani.

The gathering fell silent. All faces watched and listened for her to pronounce the infant's *best* name.

"I think I will call her Jenny," proclaimed Nani.

Vasentha let the name roll off his tongue and pronounced it a "*best* name" to a burst of applause.

"*Jaldi, jaldi,*" Vasentha commanded as he tried to get the seated children to hurry and finish their tea.

Footsteps from outside made louder and louder slaps on the hard-packed path as older children arrived from school. No one wanted to miss the spur-of-the-moment program.

The twenty-nine youngsters stood and Vasentha put one finger to his lips, the eternal sign of silence. Then he began singing, with each child following at its own tempo. He had translated the song into the *Paradhi* language.

A thunderous applause followed.

Vasentha turned to Dr. Suresh and proudly said, "They call me Sir."

From an insignificant, skinny *Paradhi* tribal boy to a leader, he had come to be called Sir; no higher honor could be given. The unimaginable had happened.

AND THE STORY CONTINUES . . .

About the Author

Sylvia H. Eckhardt, better known as SHE, is a first-time author. She lives with her husband, Loren, in Cumming, GA, and is a part-time staff member of North Point Ministries in Alpharetta, GA. Professionally; SHE is a certified interior designer still operating her own business for over thirty-five years.

Loren is Executive Director of Prakash for India and SHE is an important part of the team. They travel to India once or twice a year for accountability, encouragement, and education of staff.

It was unthinkable to her that SHE would ever write a book, but God had a different plan for her. As she struggled with the process, a young lady on a plane ride to Seattle said to her, "If you died tomorrow, would there be regret that you wrote the book or that you didn't write it?"

Committing to finishing the writing of the book of unimaginable miracles in a young tribal boy's life before she did the pen-and-ink drawings was a strain on her creative talents, but she persevered and now is proud of the results.

This book called *They Call Me Sir* is the true story of the life of one *Paradhi* tribal boy.

SHE has known him for over twenty years and is qualified to write this book. SHE is Nani.

Endnotes

1. Denotified Tribes
   From Wikipedia, the free encyclopedia
   (Redirected from Denotified tribes of India)

   Denotified Tribes (DNTs), also known
   as **Vimukta Jati**, are the tribes that were
   originally listed under the Criminal Tribes Act
   of 1871, as "Criminal Tribes" and "addicted
   to the systematic commission of non-bailable
   offences." Once a tribe became "notified"
   as criminal, all its members were required
   to register with the local magistrate, failing
   which they would be charged with a "crime"
   under the Indian Penal Code. The Criminal
   Tribes Act of 1952 repealed the notification,
   i.e. "de-notified" the tribal communities.
   This Act, however, was replaced by a series of
   Habitual Offenders Acts, that asked police to
   investigate a "suspect's" "criminal tendencies"
   and whether their occupation is "conducive to

settled way of life." The denotified tribes were reclassified as "habitual offenders" in 1959. The name "Criminal Tribes" is itself a misnomer as no definition of tribe denotes occupation, but they were identified as tribes "performing" their primary occupation. The first census was in 1871 and at that time there was no consensus or any definition of what constitutes a "tribe." The terms "tribe" and "caste" were used interchangeably for these communities.

2. *Paradhi* tribes written by T. V. Stephens, a British officer

Public pressure in villages often prevents the nomadic community from settling in villages. The community says they are driven to crime due to discrimination and the abject poverty they are in. Often landlords take advantage of this and use the *Paradhis* to carry out crimes. As a result of this bias most are unemployed or earn their livelihood as beggars in the city.

Girish Prabhune has written a book on *Paradhi* to educate people about the *Paradhi* tribe.

3. Prakash for India

Prakash for India is a nonprofit, non-denominational organization that provides Christ-centered vocational training, leadership development and life skills education to marginalized young Indian nationals.

More than 3,500 Prakash Institutes alumni now lead self-reliant, productive lives as leaders in their families, churches and communities.

35 staff, all Indian nationals, operates the Institutes.

The government of India certifies the instructors.

Prakash Institutes of India is known nationally for its quality. Students consistently excel in national trade examinations.

The current student-staff ratio of 3:1 means students receive personalized attention.

All students undergo vocational training to learn a trade, life skills training to acquire and maintain personal good health and dignity, and discipleship training to develop ideals of purpose, faith and influence.

All courses are 12-24 months long.

www.prakash4india.org.

4. Volume XII of the 1880 *Bombay Presidency Gazette*

5. Nagpur City

Nagpur, city, northeastern Maharashtra state, western India. It lies along the Nag River and is situated at the geographic centre of the country. The landscape in and around Nagpur consists of low flat-topped hills, flat tablelands, and deep, black, fertile soils in the valleys of streams and rivers. Pop approx. 2,505,665 The city was founded in the early 18th century by Bakht Buland, a Gond raja. The city, situated at the strategic junction of road, rail, and air routes from Mumbai (Bombay) to Kolkata (Calcutta) and from Chennai (Madras) to Delhi, also developed a flourishing trade sector. More recently, technology-related activities (especially software development) became more important. The end result was that Nagpur grew rapidly in size, its population doubling between 1981 and 2011.

Britannica.com

6. Vet Med Outreach

Since 1997, Prakash Institutes and its partners have sponsored an off-site Veterinary Medicine and Self-Reliant Training courses in the local villages surrounding Nagpur. Dr. Suresh Wankhede, a Prakash alumnus and a graduate of the Nagpur Veterinary Medicine College, leads the Vet-Med Outreach program.

Village students receive hands-on training in farming, raising animals, housing, health, discipleship and the Christian life.

7. North Point Ministries, Alpharetta, GA

Starting Point International copyright 2004, North Point Community Church.

Permission was given to Prakash for India for *Marathi* translation in 2007.

Starting Point is a 13-week small group study for those seeking or starting a relationship with God. It's a safe environment to ask your tough questions and move forward in your spiritual journey.

8. www.who.int/mediacentre/factsheets

For updates about Vasentha and Vet-Med Outreach go to:
www.theycallmesirbook.com

CPSIA information can be obtained
at www.ICGtesting.com
Printed in the USA
LVHW02*0616241217
560602LV00002B/3/P